# THE MOUND BUILDERS

## BY LANFORD WILSON

★

★

DRAMATISTS
PLAY SERVICE
INC.

THE MOUND BUILDERS
Copyright © 1996, Lanford Wilson
Copyright © 1976, Lanford Wilson

**All Rights Reserved**

**SPECIAL NOTE**

*For Roy London*

THE MOUND BUILDERS received its first production at Circle Repertory Company (Marshall W. Mason, Artistic Director) in New York City, on February 2, 1975. It was directed by Marshall W. Mason; the set design was by John Lee Beatty; the costume design was by Jennifer von Mayrhauser; the sound design was by Charles London and George Hansen; the slides were by Charles London and Robert Thirkield and the production stage manager was Peter Schneider. The cast was as follows:

PROFESSOR AUGUST HOWE .......................... Robert Thirkield
CYNTHIA HOWE ............................................. Stephanie Gordon
KIRSTEN ............................................................ Lauren S. Jacobs
D. K. ERIKSEN ........................................................ Tanya Berezin
DR. DAN LOGGINS ............................................... Jonathan Hogan
DR. JEAN LOGGINS ................................................ Trish Hawkins
CHAD JASKER ........................................................ John Strasberg

# ACKNOWLEDGEMENT

The author expresses his thanks to the Rockefeller Foundation for support during the writing of this play, and to Dennis Logan Schneider and Marlyn Baum for their assistance in the research, and especially to Dr. Howard Winters of the Department of Anthropology, New York University, who kindly helped with the archaeological data, spoke with the cast and production crew of THE MOUND BUILDERS and generously gave us a hint at an archaeologist's dream.

# CHARACTERS

PROFESSOR AUGUST HOWE, an archeologist, forty
CYNTHIA HOWE, his wife, thirty-five
KIRSTEN, his daughter, eleven
D.K. (DELIA) ERIKSEN, his sister, thirty-eight
DR. DAN LOGGINS, his assistant, an archaeologist, twenty-nine
DR. JEAN LOGGINS, Dan's wife, a gynecologist, twenty-five
CHAD JASKER, the landowner's son, twenty-five

# THE SCENE

August's study in Urbana is indicated only by a desk or table that can be easily incorporated into the house at Blue Shoals. When August is alone, the lights confine us to his immediate desk area. From this light he wanders, while recording, off into the dark, and back again, sitting, standing, messing with things on his desk.

As we move into the previous summer, the house around him is revealed: An old farmhouse with a large living-dining room transformed into a living-dining-working area by the archaeologists. A stairway leads off to the bedrooms, a door opens to August's office, doors lead to an unseen front porch and a back porch that might be incorporated into the set and used as a playing area for a number of the scenes. An arch allows us to see part of the kitchen, in which there is a refrigerator.

The back wall of the set serves as a screen onto which are back-projected slides from the previous summer that serve August as the backbone of his recorded notes. He need not literally control the projector.

The house is seen from August's memory of the wrecked expedition and may be represented as he sees it — not in photographs but in his mind's eye: a house that lifted up like an ark as the lake flooded the valley and floated down some great flood-struck current, wrecking in another place.

Scenes in the house are accompanied by a dense orchestration of the outside sounds, opening the house onto its surroundings. The night is filled with noises of the country and the day with the sounds of bulldozers and workmen preparing the lakebed, which will flood the valley.

## THE TIME

February in Urbana and the previous summer in Blue Shoals, Illinois — located in the extreme south of that state, in the five-state area of Kentucky, Missouri, Indiana, Arkansas, and Illinois — at the confluence of the Wabash, Cumberland, Ohio, and Mississippi Rivers.

# THE
# MOUND BUILDERS

## ACT ONE

AUGUST. *(Sits at a desk, speaking into the microphone of a small tape recorder.)* One, two, three, four, five ... *(Getting up, walking a few paces away.)* The quick gray fox jumped over ... whatever it was the quick gray fox jumped over. *(He returns to the desk, clicks off the tape, rewinds it, and clicks it on. We hear his voice repeating "...three, four, five ... the quick gray fox jumped —" He clicks the machine off, then back to record.)* Dianne ... ah ... good morning. Or, knowing your habits, I should probably say, good afternoon. *(Pause. He walks away a few paces.)* After months of procrastination, with which I'm sure you're sympathetic, I intend to go through what is left of the wreckage of last summer's expedition. *(He returns to the desk.)* You may type this up, or go out to lunch. I'll understand either. *(He touches something on the desk. The back screen is filled with a scenic photograph of a lake at morning.)* This is the lake, against which we were racing time. *(Slide: the house.)* This is the house in which we were staying. After we spent three summers of excavation *(Slide: dam construction.)* on the mounds — within earshot of the construction of the Blue Shoals Dam — *(Slide: bulldozer.)* Engineers preparing the lake bed — *(Slide: the dig.)* uncovered evidence of an extensive village site not six hundred yards from the front door *(Several slides lead us past the lake-bed construction to the house, as we hear a car stopping outside, doors slamming, and the lights of the stage begin to reveal the house in Blue Shoals.)* of the house in which we stayed. Excavation of the Jasker Village site was a salvage operation undertaken literally as the lake basin filled behind us.

CYNTHIA. *(Coming down the stairs, followed by Kirsten.)* God, I thought they'd never get here. They must have come through

Blue Shoals. *(She goes to the door.)*

CHAD.   *(Off.)* Window's been opened for a week, I was telling the professor we had a hell of a spring. Thought it wasn't gonna be any good for you folks, but it's dried up the last week.

AUGUST.   Thank God you're here. *(As Dan, Chad, and Jean enter, carrying luggage, etc.)* Everything possible has conspired to work against us.

DAN.   Girls getting to you?

AUGUST.   I'm going to have to go to the Paducah airport. How far is Paducah?

CYNTHIA.   If there is such a place.

CHAD.   About an hour.

CYNTHIA.   Auggie's sister is being dumped on us.

AUGUST.   It's nothing to talk about; just one more thing.

CYNTHIA.   Let me help with the rest of the jazz.

JEAN.   There's not much more, Dan said to travel light. Dumped on you?

CYNTHIA.   *(As they go out to the car.)* On us. Auggie's sister. *(Kirsten follows them.)*

AUGUST.   The place looks like a resort. You've never seen so many tourists in your life.

CHAD.   *(Going out to the car.)* I told him.

AUGUST.   It gets worse every year. The girls? No, the girls are fine. They pitched their tents, made a cooking pit. Every goddamned one of them is an eagle scout.

DAN.   *(He disappears for a moment, taking folders into August's office.)* Or whatever.

AUGUST.   They're happy as bugs. Ask about you and Jean every ten minutes.

DAN.   Don't say anything about Jean being pregnant, she doesn't want them pestering her.

AUGUST.   I doubt I'll see them till September. My sister is dying again; she was scraped up off the street in Cleveland; apparently the hospitals there haven't the facilities or the will. How the hell they found us here — the man came to install the telephone, ten minutes later it was ringing.

10

DAN. She's dying?

AUGUST. Of course not, and she claims poverty so — Well, it's not worth talking about.

DAN. I've never met the lady.

AUGUST. I'm afraid there's no way I can protect you from it now.

CHAD. *(Re-entering with equipment, etc.)* I had the windows opened forever. It's been a sopping spring; thought it wasn't gonna be any good for you guys, but it's cleared up some the last week.

DAN. Thank God.

AUGUST. Conditions are excellent. *(Jean, Cynthia, and Kirsten re-enter with suitcases and knapsacks.)* We've got the bulldozer lined up for day after tomorrow; you might even be ready for it.

DAN. Oh, hell, let me help.

JEAN. That's it.

AUGUST. Jean, I'm really sorry about this.

JEAN. What's wrong with her?

AUGUST. *(Speaking in Chad's presence as one might speak before a waiter.)* ... I wouldn't know.

CYNTHIA. Acute "I wouldn't know," chronic "I suspect."

AUGUST. The hospital is flying her down tomorrow, unconscious and incognito.

CYNTHIA. And collect. *(To Jean.)* You and Dan are upstairs.

KIRSTEN. You're going to hate it. It's worse than last year.

CYNTHIA. Help carry that up and please don't be impossible.

KIRSTEN. *(Going.)* If I was you, I'd have sent me to camp. *(Cynthia follows her up.)*

CHAD. You visiting again, Doctor, or you planning to stay awhile?

JEAN. No, I'm booked for the duration.

CHAD. We'll have to get her out with us.

JEAN. Don't tell me Blue Shoals swings.

DAN. Out fishing, out to the lake. *(He takes what he can carry of the baggage upstairs.)*

JEAN. No way. What happens when the lake comes in? Will you move the house?

11

CHAD.   Electric company charge you eight hundred bucks for every line you cut ... probably cost six, seven thousand to move it up the hill.

JEAN.   You couldn't build it for that.

CHAD.   Nobody'd want to either. Beams probably rotten, you couldn't get a block under it.

JEAN.   *(As she goes upstairs, followed by Cynthia.)* Is it haunted?

CYNTHIA.   Not that we've noticed.

CHAD.   *(Going upstairs.)* What do you want? You want it haunted or you want it unhaunted? I'll go either way.

AUGUST.   *(Slide: townspeople.)* Townspeople who awaited with bated breath our discovery of King Tut's tomb. *(Slide: students.)* Alleged students. We were assisted last summer by eight girls and one presumed male from Dr. Loggins's class in field archaeology. *(Slide: Cynthia.)* Ex-relation by marriage. *(Slide: campsite.)* This is the campsite of the students, pitched well out of earshot of the house. *(Slide: Cynthia.)* Ex-relation. *(Slide: Kirsten.)* Alleged daughter. *(Slide: picnic.)* Picnic. *(Slide: people playing.)* Horseplay. *(Slide: bathers.)* Horseplay at the lake. *(Slide: Cynthia.)* Horse.

DAN.   *(As he comes back downstairs, followed by Jean and Cynthia.)* Come down to the site, you've got time.

AUGUST.   I've got to talk money with some St. Louis real-estate men this evening. This isn't going to be much of a vacation for you, Jean.

DAN.   *(Leaving.)* Sure it will.

JEAN.   Sure it will.

CYNTHIA.   *(Opening refrigerator.)* Sure it will. How about a drink? *(She slams the door, effecting a blackout, except for a flashlight beam that investigates the deserted room.)*

DAN'S VOICE.   Is someone there? Hello? *(Flashlight out.)* Hello? *(Sound of a stumble. Mumbled.)* Oh, damnit. *(The flashlight comes on. Dan in pajamas gets up, goes to the lamp, turns it on.)*

CYNTHIA.   *(Entering from the door, opening a carton of cigarettes.)* Good Lord, I thought you'd be asleep hours ago.

DAN.   I was, heard the weirdest ...

CYNTHIA.   Probably the kids on the dig.

DAN.   Thought we were being burglarized.

CYNTHIA.   Not much worry about that.

DAN.   Are you just getting in? It must be two in the morning.

CYNTHIA.   Cigarettes. You working tomorrow?

DAN.   Oh, yeah, I'll be up and —

CYNTHIA.   *(Cutting him off. Reaching for the lamp switch.)* Better get to bed then. *(Blackout.)*

KIRSTEN'S VOICE.   Mother. Mother. Mommy?

AUGUST'S VOICE.   They won't hurt you. You were dreaming.

KIRSTEN'S VOICE.   They were talking.

AUGUST'S VOICE.   They're only shadows.

KIRSTEN'S VOICE.   They were talking.

AUGUST'S VOICE.   Shhhh.

KIRSTEN'S VOICE.   They were talking. *(Sundown the next evening. Chad opens the front door as Cynthia and Kirsten come downstairs.)*

CHAD.   Got a delivery for you. *(August enters, carrying Delia.)*

AUGUST.   Please don't squirm. I'm not that strong and you're not as dissipated as you'd like to believe.

DELIA.   There is no point in dragging me inside. I'm not staying —

AUGUST.   If you want to fight, wait till I set you down!

CYNTHIA.   Just here on the —

DELIA.   I'll go to a state hospital.

AUGUST.   *(Panting.)* No state has that kind of money. *(August carries Delia to a lounge.)*

DELIA.   I'm not going to die in this godforsaken Grant Wood mausoleum.

AUGUST.   *(Beat.)* Good.

DELIA.   How the hell did they find you?

AUGUST.   I was wondering.

DELIA.   You're making quite a name for yourself. That must be gratifying after all these —

AUGUST.   — I've always been satisfied to leave the limelight to those —

DELIA.   — That's the God's truth.

AUGUST.   — to those who required it.

DELIA.   *(Beat.)* Yes, well, just as well.

AUGUST.   Why were you in Cleveland?

13

DELIA.    I don't know. It was important to go to — I met someone from Cleveland, or I don't know. I was in Casablanca. Detroit with palm trees! Vile people! Vile air! Vile climate! I went to Annaba, I went to Benghazi, I met someone from Portugal, I started to go back to Lisbon, I changed my mind and went to — *(Interrupted by a violent coughing spell.)*

AUGUST.    *(Stands unmoved, watching Delia. Finally, as she relaxes.)* Where?

DELIA.    *(After relaxing. Calmly.)* Cleveland. *(Pause.)* How long did they keep me? They kept me a month, didn't they? Why?

DAN.    *(Off, calling.)* Jean?

DELIA.    I don't mean that; I'm not that bad.

JEAN.    *(From upstairs.)* I'm up, I'll be down.

AUGUST.    *(Taking medicine and papers from Chad.)* I've got instructions, yet. You were glad enough to get away.

DELIA.    They were trying to kill me in that goddamned hospital. *(Jean comes down.)*

AUGUST.    They were not trying to kill —

| | |
|---|---|
| DELIA.    Whether they were killing me through malice and intention or killing me through ignorance of medicine is immaterial. It amounts to the same torture. | DAN.    *(Entering, dirty and mildly refractory.)* What a day. Hi. Be glad you didn't come down.<br>JEAN.    Cynthia said.<br>AUGUST.    *(Handing the paper to Jean.)* Jean, can you make any sense of that? |

CHAD.    You're going to have a lot of fun with her.

KIRSTEN.    For your information, she isn't well.

CYNTHIA.    We can do very well without that.

AUGUST.    Thank you very much, Mr. Jasker.

CHAD.    Yeah, I'll see you around. *(Chad exits.)*

AUGUST.    Jean, I don't think you and Dan have had the pleasure of meeting my sister. Dan and Jean Loggins, D. K. Eriksen.

DAN.    I talked to you on the phone once.

AUGUST.    Dan's my assistant. Jean's an intern gynecologist. If you're interested in discussing medicine, I'm sure she'll listen to you.

DELIA. "D.K." Call me Delia, that's the name Dad gave me.

JEAN. I've read your books, of course.

DELIA. That was another life, Doctor.

JEAN. If you're going to call me doctor, I'll have to call you Miss Eriksen.

DELIA. You know me. I don't *meet people*.

AUGUST. You're not to be moved.

DELIA. You know quite well this is just the sort of cozily scientific, cenobitic community that'll drive me bananas.

DAN. Oh, fine. Scientific. You should see it down there. It's a mob scene.

DELIA. No, thank you.

CYNTHIA. *(Getting a glass of wine.)* Anyone else?

DAN. I'm trying to direct some jerk with a bulldozer ...

CYNTHIA. That was worth seeing.

JEAN. I saw the cars from the house.

DAN. All day long it's been a cavalcade pouring into the field. Every family from the Mississippi to the Wabash. They got their kids, they got their picnic lunches, it looks like a fucking fairground. Where you been, people? I mean, we been here twenty-four hours already. You missed Professor Howe pulling up a patch of ragweed.

CYNTHIA. I enjoy the people showing up.

DAN. Oh, sure. "What's that thing?" Well, ma'am, that *thing* is a surveyor's alidade. It sits on a tripod and you look through here and see a family from Carbondale eating fried chicken.

CYNTHIA. They go away when they find out August isn't going to let them volunteer.

DAN. A girl says, "Why did they build those mounds?" What mounds? Oh, the one over there. That they're using for a parking lot. Well, honey, we excavated that mound last summer and we found they had built that mound over ninety-three Paducah High School cheerleaders. *(Begins to roll a joint.)*

JEAN. He loves it, of course; he performs for them like a dancing bear. The girls line up for his classes. They eat him up. I don't know if they learn anything.

AUGUST. Any number of things, I'd think.

CYNTHIA. After August explains what we hope to find, the

crowd gets so bored they leave him talking to himself.

JEAN. *(Re: the medication.)* This is morning and evening — this is four times a day.

DAN. "Why did they build the mounds?"! They built the mounds for the same reason I'd build the mounds. Because I wanted to make myself conspicuous; to sacrifice to the gods; to protect me from floods, or animals; because my grandfather built mounds; because I was sick of digging holes; because I didn't have the technology to build pyramids and a person isn't happy unless he's building something.

CYNTHIA. There are people who'd be perfectly happy tearing something down.

DAN. A person isn't happy unless he's building something. Scratch a fry cook, you'll find an architect. Listen to Chad Jasker tell you about the restaurant he's going to build. I mean, he knows the kind of light fixtures he's going to have. Every society reaches the point where they build mounds. As the society becomes more sophisticated, the rationalization for building them becomes more sophisticated. For an accomplishment, honey, to bring me closer to Elysium; to leave something behind me for my grandchildren to marvel at. To say I'd built something!

AUGUST. *I.e.,* if we find out, we'll let you know.

DELIA. Jesus, dear God, but it's bleak here. Bleak, bleak, bleak, bleak…. Bleak farmland on a bleak pond by a bleak — I can't stay here, I —

AUGUST. Normally I might try to excuse her egocentric excen —

DELIA. *(Riding over.)* But my exploits are so notorious it's useless to closet my presence here and we are forced to admit that I am convalescing from a riding accident … I fell from my horse.

AUGUST. It's rather more serious than it might sound, as it was a flying horse. *(He is pouring medicine for Delia.)*

DELIA. Jean, what is he giving me? I can't breathe. They gave him something to give me, it's preventing me from —

AUGUST. The only drugs in your system are residual from your binges in Benghazi and — wherever.

DELIA.   I can't get air.

JEAN.   You're breathing perfectly normally; if you weren't getting air, you'd be turning purple, or —

DELIA.   — What the hell does a gynecologist know about cirrhosis of the liver?

JEAN.   Absolutely nothing; except that it doesn't occur in the respiratory system.

DELIA.   All right, I'm a hypochondriac, Jean. Ignore all requests for medical advice.

JEAN.   Delia, after one week in the clinic I could spot a hypochondriac at forty feet.

DAN.   *(Who has been rolling a joint; passing it to Cynthia, who takes it, and Jean, who passes it back.)* She's not on call this summer, Delia, she's taking off eighteen months to have a baby.

JEAN.   After that I might have a better idea of what I've been talking about.

DELIA.   It doesn't take eighteen months to have a baby. It takes eighteen months to have a rhinoceros.

DAN.   *(Regarding the joint. To Jean.)* Take it.

JEAN.   No, I said.

DAN.   It's not tobacco, it won't kill you.

JEAN.   Not now, thank you.

DAN.   Only girl I've ever met who's a bigger drughead than I am, she gets pregnant and goes cold turkey on me.

JEAN.   Don't mention the offspring to the girls, we don't want it generally —

DELIA.   I will not be cross-examined by a mob of swaddling adolescents.

CYNTHIA.   Never fear; they aren't allowed near the place.

JEAN.   I thought they might.

CYNTHIA.   — That's verboten. No students, no dogs.

DAN.   I mean, I can understand giving up alcohol and meat. Well, meat, but an innocent joint.

JEAN.   *(From "giving up.")* Oh, come on, really — I don't know why it should bother you; I'm the one who's straight.

CYNTHIA.   You can't give up meat. You need all the protein you can get.

JEAN.   *(Overlapping.)* No, I'm eating perfectly normally; I'm

17

just trying to avoid toxins. And you don't require nearly the amount of protein you're led to believe. We just thought we'd give it every opportunity to make its own problems.

CYNTHIA.   Don't think it won't.

DAN.   I can imagine the little bugger deprived of —

JEAN.   O.K., so it will. That's a person's prerogative; we'll try to help, and undoubtedly screw up completely. Good God, it's lousy grass anyway.

DAN.   O.K., O.K., go to bed.

JEAN.   *(Leaving.)* I am, thank you.

DELIA.   *(Overlapping.)* Get me out of this thing. I'm going to be sick.

DAN.   Where's she staying?

KIRSTEN.   Up in my room with me.

DELIA.   Oh, dear God —

DAN.   I'll take you. *(Picking Delia up and carrying her off.)* If you bite me or throw up, I'll drop you right on the floor. *(Kirsten follows them off. Beat.)*

CYNTHIA.   Is she all right?

AUGUST.   She's fine.

CYNTHIA.   I realize she's down and out; she's undoubtedly broke.

AUGUST.   I don't think so.

CYNTHIA.   And although she's not bothered to contact us more than three times in ten years, you could feel that we've neglected her —

AUGUST.   Not as much as she's neglected herself.

CYNTHIA.   Or been neglected by her reading public.

AUGUST.   I doubt she ever had much of a reading public.

CYNTHIA.   August, it is a challenge enough to maintain civilization on these summer-long bivouacs without nursing —

AUGUST.   Ignore her; Dad did. Laugh at her.

CYNTHIA.   She isn't funny. Could you at least get someone out here to look after her so —

AUGUST.   We can't begin to afford it.

CYNTHIA.   One of the girls could help —

AUGUST.   Their parents are paying a thousand dollars a head for a credit in field archaeology, not for a nursing —

CYNTHIA. They're paying to get them out of the house.

AUGUST. Jean is a practicing intern at —

CYNTHIA. — You can't expect Jean to take up residence as the —

AUGUST. Ignore her, damnit, you have enough to do. Ignore her. She doesn't like you anyway.

DAN. *(In from upstairs, out the door.)* I'm going to take a walk. The girls said someone was snooping around the dig last night. We haven't even started, we've got prowlers; I don't know what they think we're going to find. What do they think we're going to find?

CYNTHIA. *(Going upstairs.)* She likes me fine, August. She always has. It's you she can't stand.

AUGUST. *(Alone.)* Well, fine, fine, fine, good, good. *(As the slides change furiously.)* Dianne, this wreckage appears to be in a state of organization you will undoubtedly recognize as typical of my ex-wife. Please throw away those works of her genius which do not pertain to the excavation. Mrs. Howe, with stunning evidence to the contrary, persists in believing she is Diane Arbus. My sister, for instance, is of marginal archaeological interest. *(Slide: site.)* This is the rather unprepossessing site as we found it. The trial pit — stratigraphy exposed seven separate layers of occupation on the site. *(Site.)* A bulldozer was employed to remove a dense growth of weeds and about four inches of root-bearing topsoil. The remaining four to six inches of humus above the plow sole was cleared by hand and screened. *(Slide: projectile points.)* This soil proved to be the repository of Late Woodland artifacts of surpassing mediocrity which were joyfully displayed to me chip by chip. *(Six quick slides of the lake.)* This is the lake. *(As Jean comes down, dawn arrives and Chad enters.)* This is the lake. This is the lake. This is the lake. This is the lake. This is the — *(Chad framed against the lake.)*

CHAD. *(Immediately, as August stands in stunned remembrance.)* Last summer I didn't really figure you to marry Dan. You seemed to be pretty sure of what you wanted.

JEAN. Dan and I wanted more or less the same thing, I think.

CHAD.   I tell you what, I got the car out front; there's something I want to show you.

JEAN.   I don't think so.

CHAD.   — You don't even know what it is.

JEAN.   — I know, but nevertheless —

CHAD.   — You only live once.

JEAN.   I'm not sure that's been proved.

CHAD.   The courthouse. What can happen? Who's gonna miss you?

JEAN.   I've seen it.

CHAD.   Inside?

JEAN.   No, I haven't been inside.

CHAD.   — See, now, you don't know. I want to show you.

JEAN.   What?

CHAD.   Will you come?

JEAN.   No. I can't, Chad; what?

CHAD.   You'll promise to see it?

JEAN.   When I go into town again.

CHAD.   There's a model of damn near the whole county laid out — it's huge — guess what it's called. The whole model —

JEAN.   I can't guess, I really don't think —

CHAD.   *(Overlapping.)* — O.K., O.K., I'm not playing with you — you promised. It's called Jasker's Development. The Jasker Development. They got ... the hills, they got all the buildings, the mounds are on it — the ones that are left — they even got little trees set up — and this big, beautiful blue lake — like — not round, but maple-shaped, hand-shaped. We been talking six years to get Washington to give it to us.

JEAN.   The mounds that are left?

CHAD.   Four of them will be left, the other five the Interstate will take out. It's all part and parcel with the development. The lake and the new Interstate. See, we got 57 from Chicago already, which they're widening, and the new Interstate cuts across us the other way with all these interchanges and all. It all goes — aw, hell, it'll just take fifteen minutes to see the damn model and understand what's happening —

JEAN.   — No, I'm sure. You can feel it. We're an anachronism. Squint your eyes and you can already see girls water-skiing over the tops of the hawthorn trees. Restaurants with dance bands. It's all changing. The lake has become the fact, hasn't it?

CHAD. Pretty much.

JEAN. And you'll own a lot of the shoreline, won't you?

CHAD. Good piece. I could show you if we —

JEAN. — Come on, really —

CHAD. — Well, it's not how much we own, it's where it is. See — Dad was smart enough not to sell. Only thing he ever did — Guys were coming down from Memphis — See, we're sitting on the lake and the interchange.

JEAN. So you're right in the middle of it.

CHAD. We *are* the middle of it — we didn't even know. You wouldn't recognize this town if you'd seen it five years ago. Like, it didn't start being a tourist attraction till a few years ago; but all of a sudden Lily-Tulip is buying up twenty acres to build a new home office, a national headquarters with landscaping, and another one — a box company — cardboard boxes, and everybody's trying to buy our place. These guys from Memphis are talking to brokers and the brokers are driving out to chew it over with us, you know. And their offer goes up and it goes up, Dad just sits tight on it — and finally these guys come down to talk to us themselves, and they say, all right, you're not going to sell — you got the place we want to build on — what would you say about giving us a *lease*.

JEAN. Oh ... that could mean a lot more.

CHAD. Every month, month on month for as long as they're in operation. They been working over a year. Memphis is the main office of the Holiday Inn people. They've got their market studies, their books full of figures, they've got their artists'-concepts drawings already. They got their 800-unit motel, they got their swimming pools, and the facilities to the lake, they got a layout would amaze ... *(Floating)* ... Dream of something. Dream of something you want ... anything. A restaurant with twenty-four-hour service — dream of anything you want. They showed us rug samples that thick — with padding under it. See, we're sitting on the lake and the interchange.

JEAN. All first-class stuff.

CHAD.   A barber sh — ah, beauty parlor. A uh — the clubs, the little — with clubs ...

JEAN.   Sauna?

CHAD.   No, you hit the damn ball, the little setup for a —

JEAN.   Tennis court?

CHAD.   Tennis court, too, but those — oh, shit. Golf! Little golf —

JEAN.   Miniature golf.

CHAD.   No, that's kids, that's toys — Chip and putt! Chip and putt. For practicing.

JEAN.   Never heard of it.

CHAD.   It's like where you learn, you practice — *you* never heard of it! *I* never had a golf club in my *hand.* There's a golf course at Marion, eighty miles off, probably the closest place you could go — I probably couldn't hit — *(Enjoying himself, nearly laughing.)* — I'd dig up the green; they'd kick me off the — but I'm going to! Hell! Go out chipping and putting; get me a pair of the shorts and the socks and the cap and those gloves they wear — Chip and putt with the pros, man. Lee Trevino's.

JEAN.   You'll be terrific.

CHAD.   You know what we get? Three percent. On every dollar spent.

JEAN.   That's amazing; that's a lot.

CHAD.   Of everything except food. One percent on food and drink ... that's the deal they're offering us.

JEAN.   You will be rich. That's what I find so profound about politics; the grace notes of that kind of power. The signing of an energy bill in Washington transforms rural areas into resorts — field hands into busboys.

CHAD.   Yeah.

JEAN.   They shall beat their plowshares into Pontiacs.

CHAD.   *(Almost holding his breath.)* ... I ... got six acres all my own. For a house. On an island. I got an island — it will be. Out a little bit on the lake. Looks right across to it. Be able to sit on the lawn and watch people drive up off there to the motel — say that's another ten bucks. That guy over there's havin' himself a beer, that's two cents! —

JEAN. You'll get a kick out of it. *(A long pause; as she starts to move.)*

CHAD. Hey ... *(Jean stops.)* I'll give it to you.... Anything you want, it's yours. I'll sign it over. You're the only thing I ever saw I really wanted.

JEAN. *(Long pause.)* No.

CHAD. I want you to —

JEAN. — Chad — get lost. *(Cynthia enters with Kirsten.)*

CHAD. Thought I'd come over and see if you people got rained on last night.

CYNTHIA. Did we? You didn't say anything about it.

JEAN. No.

CYNTHIA. Of course no one's out at the dig till it dries up this afternoon; we're all holed up here. *(Jean leaves, Kirsten follows her.)*

CHAD. I'm gonna need some bread. About thirty dollars.

CYNTHIA. *(Beat.)* So you can have another night with the locals on rye-and-ginger?

CHAD. Come on, I got some buddies waiting for me in town. *(Cynthia reaches for her purse as they exit.)*

AUGUST. *(Alone — no slide.)* Note to myself. Separate personal from professional. Discard personal. Separate separate from separate; separate personal from imaginary, illusion from family, ancient from contemporary, etc., if possible. Organize if possible and separate if possible from if impossible. Catalogue what shards remain from the dig; celebrate separation; also, organize (a) brain, (b) photographic material, (c) letter of resignation, (d) health, (e) budget, (f) family, (f-1) family — ties, (g) life. Not necessarily in that order. Dianne, if you're still with me, copy that out and don't worry about it. *(Slide of a pot. Delia is on the lounge; Jean is repeatedly doing a sit-up exercise during the following scene. Kirsten sits watching Delia.)* This is a shell-tempered pot that we found four years ago in one of the mounds. What the hell it's doing in here only God and the photographer could tell you.

CYNTHIA. *(Entering past August.)* My eyes are driving me crazy. I don't think the muscles have the strength to focus on anything more this morning.

JEAN. Spots?

CYNTHIA. *(Falling back into a chair.)* Worse: one spot. I've been batting at a nonexistent fly all day. Everyone at the site waved at me.

JEAN. I might wander down and see how they're doing later.

CYNTHIA. They'll be up. Don't go today, it's too slow. They're digging out post molds. It takes forever and they're not uncovering anything but dark spots. *(To Delia.)* I hope you weren't cold last night; it can get pretty nippy in June, we —

DELIA. I froze.

CYNTHIA. What?

DELIA. I froze.

CYNTHIA. *(Getting up again.)* I'll get the blankets from our room. We all practically sleep outside from March to November.

DELIA. *(Overlapping from Cynthia's "all.")* I'm fine now. I'm fine now.

CYNTHIA. Do you have clothes or anything that we should send for? Other than what's in the trunk?

DELIA. What trunk?

CYNTHIA. The trunk you shipped from Oran.

DELIA. Did I? Good.

CYNTHIA. The hospital discovered your identity by redeeming the claim check on your trunk.

DELIA. That's — resourceful of them.

CYNTHIA. Do you have anything that —

DELIA. Don't worry about it.

CYNTHIA. We're so schizophrenic since we've been coming down here. Just as I begin adjusting to a life stripped down to what I can carry on my back we —

JEAN. — pull up camp —

CYNTHIA. — migrate back to eleven rooms of memorabilia.

JEAN. I don't think Delia's a collector.

DELIA. I collect with one hand and mislay with the other. The world's unclaimed-baggage departments are crammed with my paraphernalia.

CYNTHIA. I know it's going to sound fatuously supportive, but you're looking better. How are you feeling?

DELIA. Better.

JEAN. Don't rub your eyes.

CYNTHIA. Oh, I know ...

DELIA. Don't stare at the Gorgon, Kirsten; you'll turn to stone.

CYNTHIA. You have a fan.

KIRSTEN. Where's Oran?

DELIA. Tunisia — Algeria.

JEAN. That sounds very glamorous to us landlubbers.

DELIA. It isn't. Oran was Camus's model for the *locus in quo* of *The Plague*. We were host to every fly on the Mediterranean.

KIRSTEN. Were you there with your husband?

CYNTHIA. Kirsten, she isn't married anymore, you know that.

DELIA. *(Simultaneously.)* Good God, I haven't been married since before you were born. I don't even remember being married. I can't believe — *(Trailing into laugh.)*

KIRSTEN. You remember being —

DELIA. — I was very young, darling; I was terrified of rejection; what I remember is an anxiety to please so severe I could hardly fight down the panic long enough to get drunk. I was bonded, I wasn't — *(Coughs.)*

KIRSTEN. You don't remember what he looked like?

CYNTHIA. Honey, don't bother her.

DELIA. No, it's fine — He was a strong, hirsute, sweating, horny cocksman. He sold drilling equipment. I was so captivated that that didn't strike me as funny until years after I got out from under him.

KIRSTEN. I thought he was an artist.

DELIA. God, no, God, no— God no! He had not eyes in his head! We traveled through the East. He traveled, I trailed.

JEAN. You were working, though.

DELIA. Self-defense.

KIRSTEN. New England or the Far East?

DELIA. Egypt, Lebanon, Syria, Cyprus, Metaxa, Ouzo, Grappa, Cinzano ...

AUGUST. *(Off.)* ... as long as it's considered subservient to anthropology. We'll never have sufficient clout till we have a separate autonomous department.

DAN. *(As he and August enter.)* Man, it's hotter than a pistol out there. *(August goes to his office, Dan to the refrigerator.)*

CYNTHIA. Tell me about it.

KIRSTEN. And you split.

CYNTHIA. Don't bother her Kirsten —

DELIA. And I split. But once set in motion, the moving object tends to remain in motion.

CYNTHIA. Well, maybe the stationary object now will tend to remain stationary.

DELIA. Couldn't do that. Couldn't do that. I have a very real terror of gathering moss. *(Dan opens a beer.)*

CYNTHIA. I don't know how you stay thin —

JEAN. I'll catch up with him.

DAN. *(To Delia.)* I think I might welcome a little moss after your experiences.

DELIA. After how many years? Eight, nine —

JEAN. Don't, I'm counting —

DELIA. — After living in the liquid world, wouldn't I welcome being washed up onto some sandy lakeshore-front property in the sun to dry out. Out in the thin air where the hand is quicker than the eye and noises are distinct and occur at their source rather than inside your head. Well, I'm — vaguely conscious of allowing myself to float up toward the surface — at least to look around.

CYNTHIA. Good.

DELIA. Whereupon I'm certain I'll want to drown myself.

DAN. Again.

JEAN. *(Giving up the exercises.)* Oh. Uncle. A hundred ten.

KIRSTEN. Up toward the surface to look around.

DELIA. Hello. Good morning What's for breakfast? I hope you weren't cold last night.

JEAN. Is that O.K.?

DAN. *(Looking through typed pages.)* All that only typed up to four pages?

JEAN. How are the post molds coming?

DAN. "Post molds"? You've been reading books.

JEAN. Talking to Cynthia.

DAN. *(To Cynthia.)* We're ready on the third section while the girls are taking a lunch break if you want to get at it.

CYNTHIA. They can wait.

JEAN. What were the posts for?

CYNTHIA. Walls. You've never seen so many holes in your life.

DAN. These are for the walls of a roundhouse. They set posts around in a circle about every two feet then filled in the walls with mud and dabble. Walls about yea thick — fire pit in the middle — no chimney, only one door — must have been smoky as hell. Men only — sat around telling hunting stories.

CYNTHIA. Then there must be about forty houses.

DAN. We won't get to them all, just a general configuration.

JEAN. This isn't really a typical village, is it?

DAN. Oh, yeah, pretty much.

CYNTHIA. Boringly so.

JEAN. In your notes you say that the typical village configuration is a large plaza with a mound at each end —

DAN. The downtown area. A mound for the high muck-a-muck God-King, and a mound for the temple.

JEAN. — and a street running around the plaza with houses all around the four sides of the plaza, all very geometrically laid out.

DAN. Very good. Roundhouse we're working on is down here in the corner.

JEAN. Swell. Only where are the mounds in the middle of the plaza?

KIRSTEN. Jasker plowed them under.

DAN. They were plowed under. That's why we didn't know there was a village here.

JEAN. And they weren't burial mounds so who would know —

DAN. No, burial mounds aren't associated with a village. They're a lot earlier. Burial mounds were built by hunters and gatherers; they didn't have a permanent village. There weren't any villages to speak of until the Mississippian Culture moved into the area and began to develop agriculture.

27

CYNTHIA.   Then they had to hang around the house and tend the fields — sacrifice to the gods of harvest and what-not.

DAN.   There's been at least three different cultures who built mounds in the area — the Adena, back around 600 B.C.

JEAN.   B.C.? 600 B.C.?

CYNTHIA.   Don t ask; you don't want to know.

DAN.   600 B.C. Then the Hopewell Culture. They both built burial mounds. Then along about A.D, 700 a whole new people moved into the area, and instead of building burial mounds, they built a mound and on top of the mound built a temple. Two mounds. One for their temple and one for their God-King.

JEAN.   One at each end of the plaza.

DAN.   And we call these people the Temple Mound People. Or for short, the Early Mississippian Culture.

JEAN.   And those are our guys.

CYNTHIA.   All very filled with pomp and circumstance.

JEAN.   Cahokia, up in St. Louis, was one of the Mississippian cities, wasn't it?

DAN.   Yeah. Probably forty, fifty thousand. Bigger than Paris or London at the time.

JEAN.   I know, I was reading your book on it.

DAN.   I knew it; let me tell you, don't read books.

JEAN.   Do you get the feeling that they were just the least bit weird?

CYNTHIA.   Oh, definitely.

JEAN.   There's a grave with six men all laid out ceremonially, with their right hands chopped off.

CYNTHIA.   You find that all the time.

JEAN.   Well, I mean, really. Do they have an explanation for that?

CYNTHIA.   Maybe they were caught abusing themselves. (Beat.) Where's your book on circulation? I haven't seen you crack a medical book since you've been here.

JEAN.   What's more immediate is a stack of articles I've intended to read for three months.

CYNTHIA.   Well, don't hire out as a typist. August spends

half his time drumming up money to hire secretaries to type Dan's notes.

JEAN.   You don't know how ignorant I am about the —

CYNTHIA.   Well, stay that way. I'm not joking. Don't start. *(To Dan.)* Have one of the girls do it. *(To Jean.)* It's a full-time job and you already have one.

JEAN.   Two.

DAN.   *(Unfazed by anything.)* I'd do it myself but I can't type and I can't spell.

JEAN.   What will you do after the Interstate levels the mounds you're supposed to dig next summer?

AUGUST.   *(Off, calling.)* — Dan? Where'd you put it?

DAN.   *(Laying down pages.)* Where'd I put what?

CYNTHIA.   Really, don't bother with it.

DAN.   *(Giving Jean a pat in passing.)* That's terrific. Come down later.

JEAN.   Oh, God. I don't mind correcting your spelling, but please don't pat me on the head.

DAN.   *(Laughing, going into the office.)* Where'd I put what? *(He shuts the door behind him.)*

CYNTHIA.   Have you learned anything about pregnancy that's going to revolutionize childbirth?

JEAN.   Oh ... no. The source of that smug glow pregnant women have. You really do feel the miracle of it all. Every woman is the only woman who's ever been pregnant. That — and one moment of blinding damnation that was probably singular to me. After two immediate miscarriages and all kinds of anxiety about it —

CYNTHIA.   I didn't realize you'd —

JEAN.   Well, as grandmother would say, "Our women have a history of it" — That's why I'm reluctant to accept premature congratulations. Still, when I finally managed to stay pregnant for two months and told Dan that maybe we were O.K. — I felt for one second that in telling him I had breached a covenant between me and the baby. As though I had — forever fallen from grace. Did you feel that?

CYNTHIA.   Fallen from grace, I wouldn't remember; the miracle, yes.

AUGUST. *(Re-entering with Dan.)* But that has nothing to do with us.

DAN. Just tell them we've thought of calling the dig the First National Bank of Carbondale Village.

AUGUST. That would do it. Kirsten's coming along and trying to look deprived.

KIRSTEN. I think we do better when I look hopeful.

DAN. *(To Jean.)* Come down and dig out a post mold with us. *(Delia laughs.)*

JEAN. It doesn't sound very romantic. It's more — what — rural than the spectacular cultures, isn't it?

AUGUST. It was quite spectacular — take her up to the Koster Site.

JEAN. I mean like the Aztec Empire.

DAN. The Aztec culture was not really an empire.

JEAN. Well, or the Incan culture.

AUGUST. The Incans had an empire. We'd be working somewhere else if our work here wasn't important.

DAN. If Cortes had landed here in 1250, you wouldn't be talking about the Aztecs at all; you'd be talking about the glory that was Jasker's Field. They had longer trade routes — they just didn't leave anyone around to translate their poetry

JEAN. They had poetry?

AUGUST. I would imagine. Poetry, drama — the Aztecs did.

JEAN. Do we know any of it? The Aztec —

AUGUST. Yes, otherwise we —

JEAN. What did it sound like?

AUGUST. *(To Cynthia.)* I'll give you a ring about five. *(He exits.)*

DAN. Free verse, rhyming verse; think Emily Dickinson:
> Here are our precious flowers and songs
> May our friends delight in them,
> May the sadness fade out of our hearts.
> This earth is only lent to us.
> We shall have to leave our fine work.
> We shall have to leave our beautiful flowers.
> That is why I am sad as I sing for the sun.

DELIA. Who was that?

DAN.   We don't know his name, Delia. We only know his work. *(He exits.)*

CYNTHIA.   *(Picking up her equipment as Jean begins exercising.)* Do you really think you'll go on with a medical career after you have the baby?

JEAN.   *(Stops dead. Beat.)* It didn't stop you. You managed. Don't rub your —

CYNTHIA.   I have several thousand photographs of Kirsten. Maybe you'll go into pediatrics. *(Pause.)* If you come down, bring a hat; the sun's murder. *(Starts out.)*

JEAN.   Were you into a photographic career before —

CYNTHIA.   *(Overlapping.)* Not at all, not at all. I'm sorry I brought it up. *(Jean goes to the door as Cynthia leaves.)*

JEAN.   *(After Cynthia has gone, looking after her.)* Oh, brother.

DELIA.   Did they fight? *(Jean looks around to her.)* The Temple Mound people?

JEAN.   *(Not really thinking about it.)* Apparently. When they came — I think everyone would like to agree that they were runaways from the Toltecs, but haven't found substantial correlation; the books are all very careful about sweeping pronouncements, but it's all looking like a mud version of the Toltecs — so when they came up they fought off whoever was here. And built the first fortifications and all that. Probably kept the first slaves.

DELIA.   You feed it all into a computer — all the facts and fancies the doctors have printed or typed or brushed and the computer would print out NOTHING APPLIES. It doesn't scan. The truth is in dreams and nightmares, but you haven't succeeded in getting that down. Rank was the ultimate genius, sure, but he couldn't tell you how to keep from cutting your wrist while you're shaving your legs.

JEAN.   So you stopped shaving your legs.

DELIA.   Cause and — *(Coughs.)*

JEAN.   *(Beat.)* Effect. I wouldn't think you'd have much faith in computers.

DELIA.   Well — "faith" …

JEAN.   Exactly.

DELIA.   It's all going to be facts, Doctor. Art is part of a primitive culture, really. The future is photography. We won't have time for anything more subtle than lies.

JEAN. You have a way of conveying the impression you know all the answers.

DELIA. The answer to which is, Yes, but I don't know any of the questions.

JEAN. Neat.

DELIA. Isn't that neat? It's a lie, but it's neat. I know the questions by rote. I just don't stand up well under them.

JEAN. No, neither do I. I won the spelling bee when I was a kid. Did beautifully, then had a complete collapse.

DELIA. I'd think so.

JEAN. Learned a lot of words.

DELIA. That's usually enough for a good impression. Spelling bee? God.

JEAN. *The* spelling bee. When I was what? Twelve. National Champion.

DELIA. Dear God.

JEAN. No one in the neighborhood went to the dictionary, they all came to me. I was tutored by my grandmother so I was the only kid who used the old-fashioned English grammar school method of syllable spelling. Charmed the pants off them. It started out as a kind of phenomenon or trick — then when my teachers realized they had a certifiable freak on their hands, they made me study for it.

DELIA. We're all freaks — all us bright sisters.

JEAN. It wasn't so bad until the competitions started. I mean, it wasn't like the little girl practicing her violin with her nose against the window pane, watching all the other little girls at play. But I managed to work it into a nervous breakdown. *(Pause.)* I couldn't stop. Every word that was said to me, I spelled in my head *(In an easy, flowing, but mechanical rhythm.)* Mary, go to bed. Mary go to bed. Mary. M-A-R-Y. Mary. Go. G-O. Go. Mary go. To. T-O. To. Mary go to. Bed. B-E-D. Bed. Mary go to bed. Mary go to bed: M-A-R-Y-G-O-T-O-B-E-D. Mary, go to bed.

DELIA. Mary?

JEAN. Mary Jean. *(She wanders to the door to gaze out.)* That, and I lost the meaning. Mary, go to bed was syllables, not sense. *(Beat.)* Then there were days when the world and its objects separated, disintegrated into their cellular structure, molecular — worse — into their atomic structure. And nothing held its form. The air was the same as the trees and a table was no more substantial than the lady sitting at it.... Those were ... not good days.

DELIA.   I don't imagine. But you got it together.

JEAN.   Oh, yes. Juvenile resilience.

DELIA.   And that led one directly into gynecology.

JEAN.   That led one directly into an institution, and contact with some very sick kids. Some of them more physically ill than neurotic — who were not being particularly well cared for; and that led to an interest in medicine. And reading your books and others at an impressionable age led to gynecology. *(Beat.)* Also, living with my grandmother and her cronies, who were preoccupied with illness, kept it pretty much in my curiosity. They were always talking about friends with female troubles, problems with their organs. Of course, the only organ I knew was at church. I developed a theory of musical instruments as families. The cello was the mother, the bass was the father, and all the violins were the children. And the reason the big father organ at Grace Methodist Church made such a mournful sound was that female organs were always having something wrong with them.

DELIA.   Round John Virgin.

JEAN.   Exactly.

DELIA.   Have you seen Dad's book on the eye? Vision, actually?

JEAN.   I didn't know he had one. He was a doctor?

DELIA.   Physiologist. Hated practicing physicians. Eye, ear, nose, throat.

JEAN.   Somewhat different field.

DELIA.   I'd guess. The downstairs of the house was his, his consultation room, his office, his examination rooms: big square masculine Victorian rooms with oversized charts of the musculature of the neck and diagrams of the eye with the retina and rods and cones and iris and lens and those lines projected out into space indicating sight. And it appeared to me — still does — that rather than the eye being a muscle that collects light, those beams indicated that the eye projects vision onto the outside. *(Pause.)*

JEAN.    The place has changed since last year. I came down a couple of times last summer — weekends — watching their progress. But something odd is happening now — or not happening. There's something ... I don't think it's the pregnancy, I think it's *here*. Or maybe my eyes are just projecting vision onto the outside.

DELIA.    No, I don't think that's quite it.

JEAN.    I have an intense desire to turn to the end of the chapter and see how it all comes out. You don't happen to have a deck of tarot on you, do you?

DELIA.    No, I just look that way.

JEAN.    It's only an anxiety.

DELIA.    Generally speaking, Jean, ignore the Ides of March, but beware soothsayers. *(Jean laughs.)* The old woman in *Dombey and Son* comes upon Edith in a lonely wood and says: "Give me a shilling and I'll tell your fortune." And Edith, of course, cuts her dead and goes on — Edith cuts everyone dead. And the old woman screams: "Give me a shilling or I'll yell your fortune after you."

JEAN.    Oh, God. I'd pay. God, would I pay.

DELIA.    That's what I thought.

JEAN.    Jesus. Would I ever. What was the fortune? *(Pause.)* What was the —

DELIA.    Give me a shilling or I'll tell you.

JEAN.    Don't! Don't do that. What was the fortune?

DELIA.    Uh, someone intervened.

JEAN.    The hero.

DELIA.    The villain actually.

JEAN.    Do you do that? Turn to the end of a book to find out —

DELIA.    No, I don't — I don't read anymore.

JEAN.    You do, of course. What's wrong is this inaction. I'm used to doing things. The university funds a clinic, you can't imagine. Coming off that is like coming off speed.

DELIA. And that's your answer. Why do you want to be a doctor when we get such a kick from diagnosing our own case? What seems to be the problem, Mrs. Blue — "Well, Doctor, I'm afraid I'm going to require twenty-five 300-milligram capsules of Declomycin."

JEAN. Oh, it's true. A gargle and forty Ornade spansules.

DELIA. Jean's only coming down off work and D.K. is frantically beating the bushes for something to believe in. Something with passion to warm up the blood and make her forget where it hurts. Great blinders is believing in and she's a great believer in blinders.

JEAN. Where does it hurt, D.K.?

DELIA. Doctor, it's a pain in the ass.

JEAN. Where does it hurt, D.K.?

DELIA. I thought we agreed not to ask. *(Blackout — slide utterly black with a hint of fire somewhere.)*

AUGUST. I think this would be the tribal weenie roast.

CHAD'S VOICE. *(Drunk, pounding the door.)* Goddamn! Cynthia?

CYNTHIA'S VOICE. *(Harsh whisper.)* What are you doing? The house is full of people, none of whom have ever been known to sleep!

CHAD'S VOICE. *(Drunk, urgent.)* I gotta go. I had to come over. I had to come.

CYNTHIA'S VOICE. Shhhhhh! Good God, are you drunk?

CHAD'S VOICE. I drunk thirty dollars' worth of rye-and-ginger since six o'clock.

CYNTHIA'S VOICE. Oh, God. Come outside.

CHAD'S VOICE. When you need it, we go. We gotta go when I need it, damnit.

CYNTHIA'S VOICE. Come outside; come on outside.

CHAD'S VOICE. *(Louder, insistent.)* I'm hot, baby — get down; take it, goddamnit; it'll just be ten seconds; nobody's gonna come in in ten seconds.

CYNTHIA'S VOICE. Shhhh. Come on.

CHAD'S VOICE. Come on.

CYNTHIA'S VOICE. Shh. Come on, come outside. *(The screen-door spring sounds as they are heard to go outside. Flashlight.)*

DAN. Is someone there? Hello? *(Flashlight out.)* Hello? *(Stumbles.)* Oh, goddamnit. *(Flashlight on, he's on his knees, the light finds the lamp, he turns it on. Delia is on the lounge, a hand averting the light from her eyes.)* Oh. Oh! Shit. Oh, baby. Oh, wow! I'm sorry. Oh, Jesus ... I thought we were being burglarized.... Oh, you scared the piss out of me. *(He sits down.)*

DELIA. *(Still with her hand averting the light. Flatly.)* Any time.

DAN. Couldn't you have coughed or something? Were you asleep?

DELIA. No.

DAN. Woooooooow! You expect to see someone. Then you do see someone. Wow! You couldn't sleep?

DELIA. I don't know.

DAN. I'm a light sleeper.

DELIA. *(Only a glance at him.)* Why don't you straighten up like a man? Your posture is a disgrace to the species.

DAN. That's probably from working in —

DELIA. — Oh, for godsake, put your shoulders down, you look like a capon. I'm not talking about your physical health. I'm talking about this Howdy-Dowdy, hale-fellow, nice-guy, in-nocent-babe-in-the-woods facade you splash over every — I'm a writer, I'm not a chiropractor.

DAN. You still think of yourself as a writer? *(Delia looks at him directly for the first time.)* I mean, I'm glad; are you working? Are you writing? You know, I knew August for two years before I knew you were his sister? We read you at school ... Contemporary American Lit. Professor ... can't remember. Read half your second book aloud. Second one was *Spindrift?* *(Pause.)* He was wild about it. Read everything aloud because he knew (a) we wouldn't read anything he assigned, and he had this thing that any really good book should be read aloud (b). *(He begins rolling a joint.)*

DELIA. Sounds like a lousy disciplinarian.

DAN. Frustrated actor. Read terrifically.

DELIA. Snap course.

DAN. No shit; that's all I took my last year.

DELIA. Where was this?

DAN. Columbia. Said you were the last defender of a

36

woman's right to make a fool of herself.

DELIA. Oh, surely not the last. Tell him I was drunk.

DAN. When you wrote it? Does that make it bad?

DELIA. No. It makes it easier. No, it doesn't. Nothing makes it easier — *(Mumbles, a light cough.)*

DAN. What?

DELIA. *(Forced out.)* I said nothing makes it easier once it starts becoming difficult! Half of it. Half of it should read very nicely. Half of it was dictated into a tape recorder. Because I couldn't find the typewriter — keys.

DAN. I liked it.

DELIA. The half you heard.

DAN. I read it. I liked it a lot. I realize you couldn't care less one way or the other whether I —

DELIA. *(Overlapping almost from "realize.")* I had a little secretary come in from some agency and type it for me. Temporary help. She looked ... "temporary." Very neat, sweet, meek. She typed eight hours a day for five days, never misspelling a word, stacked the manuscript on the desk, put on her neat, sweet, meek gloves while I wrote out a check; took her check sweetly, put on her coat meekly, and left by the front door neatly. And I took the manuscript, put it in a box, wrapped it in vinegar and brown paper, addressed it to my publisher, who had been expecting it daily for over five months, threw it on the closet floor, and got drunk for three days. Wouldn't answer the phone.

DAN. Because it was finished?

DELIA. Because I thought she hadn't liked it.

DAN. *(Pause.)* And after three days?

DELIA. The police, with my publisher, broke the door in. I told him it was going to be a failure. Later on he told me the book was a success but I was a failure.

DAN. I liked it very much. *(Beat. He gets up, looking out again.)* Was that you? That clamor down here?

DELIA. You've been coming here four summers? You and Auggie and Cynthia? I'd think you'd have noticed that you're in the country out here. The natives get restless at night. The dogs raid the hen houses. They get hungry.

37

DAN. *(Offering the joint.)* Want a toke?

DELIA. How did you ever survive four years in New York?

DAN. Five, I got my M.S. *(Delia laughs.)* It was really intimidating, but I kinda loved it. I had this great roommate who worried about me. Thought he was Seymour Glass. The guy in all the —

DELIA. I'm familiar —

DAN. Studied medieval history, but he was a nice guy —

DELIA. — Well, though, medieval history isn't something to cross off lightly, he could have told you how the Flemish used a virgin to distract the horny unicorn.

DAN. We used to put him on.

DELIA. Yes, I'm sure —

DAN. — Well, then, also, I really believed the only way to feel completely safe on the sidewalks of New York is to be completely, knockdown drunk. I mean visibly, stinking, reeling, dangerously drunk.

DELIA. How many times have you been dangerously —

DAN. On the sidewalks of New York? Once. But it's the only time I felt safe. I was badly drunk. In a bad drunk way.

DELIA. I'm familiar. Sick drunk.

DAN. Sick doesn't even begin. I saw signs, sidewalks, people veering out of my way. Taxis *avoiding* me. I fell off the curb — had no idea what it was — got up, staggered across the street wondering where all the *buildings* had gone — realized just as I got to the other side that probably I was crossing a street — looked around to confirm it, and fell over the other curb. *(Pause.)* In the rain. I remember walking up to a street light. I thought it was a street light, it wasn't a street light, I thought it was a street light, and wrapping my arms around it like it was my mother. Cold hard wet beautiful mother. Stood there forever. Long enough to lose all orientation. Finally opened my eyes and right at my nose this sign says: "You must answer to get help." *(Pause.)* White letters on a red field. "You must answer to get help." Blackout. Next thing I know, my roommate's shaking me awake asking me what time I got in. I said, "You must answer to get help." *(Pause.)* You ever see that sign? *(Pause.)* "You must answer ..."

DELIA.  I missed that one.

DAN.  One on every block. I saw it about a month later. Old friend. Little letters:  "Break glass; lift receiver; answer operator." Big print: "You *must* answer to get help." No more metaphysical than anything else in this world. *(Pause.)* Fire-alarm box. One on every block. *(Pause, looks at her. Delia stares blankly off into space.)* Friend of man and dog. *(Long pause. He gets up, reaches for the lamp.)* Light on or off? *(Pause.)* Delia? D.K.? ... light on or off? *(A pause. He turns off light. Blackout.)*

AUGUST.  *(Slide: Mr. Jasker.)* This is old man Jasker himself. The wise old bird who owns the place. After being made famous with the arrival of the college, he was looking forward to being made rich by the arrival of the lake and Interstate 64. We see him twice each year, on our arrival and departure. This is a June hello — there was no September goodbye this summer. *(Slide: the moon.)* This is the moon. *(Delia is seated in the shadows. Chad and Dan are noisily divesting themselves of rods, reels, creels, etc. Enjoying the noise; oblivious of the silence of the house. Dan goes to the refrigerator.)*

DAN.  Nothing!

CHAD.  Nothing?

DAN.  Nothing to drink. Do you want to eat?

CHAD.  God, no —

DAN.  Food?

CHAD.  Never again in my life. *(He has found a bottle of Scotch.)*

DAN.  Well, then there's nothing.

CHAD.  You call that nothing?

DAN.  Are you crazy; you want to kill yourself?

CHAD.  No — you go. "Beer on whiskey — mightly." Mightly?

DAN.  Mightly?

CHAD.  What is it? You say it.

DAN.  You're saying it. I don't know what —

CHAD.  I'm telling you, it's an old wives' tale — there's a *thing* — a saying that tells you how to judge.

DAN.  A what? What's the thing?

CHAD.  A thing. You're the educated member of the family — you're supposed —

DAN.  But not in FOLKLORE! Not in —

CHAD.   I'm not talking —

DAN.   — Absolute blind spot in folklore!

CHAD.   I'm talking words — it's a epigram or epitaph or aphorism or anagram.

DAN.   Axiom.

CHAD.   It's not an axiom.

DAN.   Well, what is it? Is it —

CHAD.   It's not a goddamned axiom. It's an easy word — it's a word! It's a saying — a truth!

DAN.   That's the word. It's a truth.

CHAD.   It's a truth, but that's not the word — ANYWAY!

DAN.   Anyway. How does it go? Tell us! Are we safe? Will we survive?

CHAD.   It goes ... *(Pauses, trying to frame it.)*

DAN.   *(Under.)* How does ...

CHAD.   *(Under.)* Just cool it a minute, will you? It goes: *(Headline.)* "BEER. ON WHISKEY."

DAN.   Sounds bad.

CHAD.   "MIGHTY RISKY ... WHISKEY. ON BEER. NEVER FEAR."

DAN.   *(Pause.)* It's an aphorism.

CHAD.   So. *(Pours a glass each.)* Whiskey on beer — *(Toast.)*

DAN.   Cheers.

CHAD.   WHISKEY ON BEER ...

DAN.   That's what I said: "Never fear."

CHAD.   Cheers. *(They drink.)*

DAN.   This will probably kills us.

CHAD.   Hey! Have you ever seen anything as beautiful as that moon?

DAN.   Never.

CHAD.   As big?

DAN.   Never. When's the harvest moon?

CHAD.   October.

DAN.   Only the harvest moon.

CHAD.   November.

DAN.   Only the harvest moon.

CHAD.   October.

DAN.   Only the harvest moon.

CHAD.   September.

DAN.   As golden?

CHAD.   Never.

DAN.   What is it? June 21, 23 — that's the summer solstice — moon.

CHAD.   *(Simple.)* It's a full moon.

DAN.   It's a full moon.

CHAD.   And you're full of shit.

DAN.   I'm fulla beer.

CHAD.   I gotta piss. *(He goes out the door.)*

DAN.   *(Alone.)* What'd we do?

CHAD.   *(Off.)* Twelve.

DAN.   Twelve's ass. I caught five and you caught what?

CHAD.   *(Off.)* You caught five, I caught seven.

DAN.   They be all right out in that tub?

CHAD.   *(Off.)* You want to clean 'em?

DAN.   Hell, I couldn't clean me.

CHAD.   *(Off.)* You better manage it; Jean'll kick your ass out on the floor.

DAN.   Hell she will. *(He stands, miming rod: casting, catch.)* Strike! Shitfire! Strike! Get the net!

CHAD.   *(Off.)* What?

DAN.   Get the net, goddamnit, I got another one!

CHAD.   *(Off.)* Get your own damn net; I got a seven-pounder out here.

DAN.   *(Dropping it.)* He who brags about size of meat — I forget what it was, but Confucius said something very appropriate to that. What'll it weigh? The big one. Five pounds?

CHAD.   *(Off.)* Six.

DAN.   Was that one motherfuckin' fish? Was that a *fight*? To the *death*?

CHAD.   *(Entering.)* That was a fight to the death.

DAN.   Was that the biggest bass you ever saw in your life?

CHAD.   No.

DAN.   Shit.

CHAD.   No.

DAN.   You've seen a bigger bass?

CHAD.   I've seen a bigger bass.

41

DAN.   Drink your beer.

CHAD.   I gotta get my ass home.

DAN.   Would you drink your damn beer?

CHAD.   You better get your duds off; get up to that warm bed, you're gonna be diggin' tomorrow.

DAN.   Terrific. You know why? 'Cause what's happening is, it's all gone wrong. And that's always very terrific.

CHAD.   Get up and have your girl give you a rubdown, huh?

DAN.   Everything's looking like a typical village, right? And all of a sudden it's not typical any more. They got something under the roundhouse.

CHAD.   Isn't that right?

DAN.   We don't know what yet. What?

CHAD.   You gotta get up to your girl.

DAN.   She's beautiful, isn't she?

CHAD.   She is that.

DAN.   And bright — you wouldn't believe it.

CHAD.   No, I'm counting on it. Let's take you up, put you to bed.

DAN.   And sweet; you wouldn't believe it.

CHAD.   No, I'm a believer.

DAN.   You better believe it.

CHAD.   Let's get you up to bed, come on.

DAN.   I'm all wet.

CHAD.   Come on.

DAN.   I'm all wet, come on.

CHAD.   Well, you said it.

DAN.   Drink your — Scotch.

CHAD.   Wore your life preserver, didn't you? That's nice out there, just you and me, huh?

DAN.   Beautiful.

CHAD.   Wouldn't be right with no one else, huh?

DAN.   No way.

CHAD.   You gettin' warm?

DAN.   I'm fine.

CHAD.   *(Very close to Dan.)* You gonna be O.K.?

DAN.   I am.

CHAD.   *(Pulling Dan closer.)* You sure? You sure?

DAN.    Yeah, well, I didn't drown, I can survive without mouth-to-mouth resuscitation.

CHAD.    Huh?

DAN.    I'm fine.

CHAD.    You know why you didn't drown — because you got a cork head!

JEAN.    *(Entering.)* You've got to be kidding; it's one-thirty in the morning.

DAN.    *(Whispering.)* Oh, damn! No! It's the night of nights! People should be up.

JEAN.    Do you drink when you're out fishing? No wonder people go fishing. *(To Delia.)* Are you all right? I mean, are they bothering you?

DELIA.    Not at all.

DAN.    Jesus Christ! I might have sat on you! We're all here. *(To Jean, moving toward her.)* This is the night —

JEAN.    Shhh! The night of nights; I hear you. Come on, really. I'm all over calamine lotion ... I'm itching all —

DAN.    Gently, gently, gently — *(Softly, singing, waltzing her gently a few steps.)* "We're gonna fill an ocean of calamine lotion ..."

JEAN.    Come on, you'll wake me up; you'll wake me — *(Breaks off.)* Oh, well, hell, it's too late; I'm awake. Damn. Damn. Damn. Are you sure we won't bother you? Were you sleeping out here?

DELIA.    No, you won't bother me. No, I wasn't sleeping.

JEAN.    *(Opening refrigerator.)* You hungry? I'm starved.

DAN.    Is anybody hungry? No one is hungry.

DELIA.    Whattaya say, Jasker?

JEAN.    What are you drinking? Is that straight Scotch?

DAN.    Well, yeah, it's.... We're sipping.

CHAD.    I'm gonna leave you all to your dig.

DAN.    Stay. Stay.

CHAD.    Later. *(Leaving.)*

DAN.    Stay awhile. *(Chad is gone.)* Eat! We'll all eat! What's the matter with him? *(Jean is making a sandwich.)*

DELIA.    What's he got on you?

DAN.    Got on me? Nothing. What are you talking about, he's not got anything on me. I owe him my life — he's not got anything on me.

DELIA.  Nobody owes their life to —

DAN.  Well — some things you don't know, do you? He pulled me out of the drink last summer. We were rowing out; I was pulling back on the oar, it came out of the socket, hit me right in the face — I passed out and slid over the side in twenty feet of water.

JEAN.  You're really too much.

DAN.  Pulled me out by the hair of my head.

JEAN.  What did you catch?

DAN.  Oh! Incredible!

JEAN.  Come on.

DAN.  (Whispers.) Four very friable, skillet-size bass. And one — mammoth ...

DELIA.  Motherfucking.

DAN.  Motherfucking President of the Lake. Come and look!

JEAN.  No, I haven't got any —

JEAN.     — It's wet! I'm barefoot. I hate fish. I mean, I'll eat it, I'm glad you caught it, but I don't like live fish.

DAN.  Come out and look. Come — Would you come out here and look.

DAN.  What do you do when they got no sense af adventure?

JEAN.  How big?

DAN.  Very big. Formidable. Six pounds. If she hadn't been here, I'd of said twelve. But a fighter! A very ... vicious opponent. Only six pounds, but solid muscle. Look at the moon at least — come look at the moon, you can see the moon from here; you don't have to even — where'd it go? (He has taken her arm.)

JEAN.  You're soaking wet. Did you fall in?

DAN.  I jumped in. I wanted to test my life jacket.

JEAN.  Did it work?

DAN.  Uh ... inconclusive. Anyway! I thought we were getting a late start. I mean, what do I know, right? But it was hot. And bass are hedonists. When it's hot on top they puddle about down at the bottom, doing whatever they do when it's

hot on top. You got to know the psychology of the mothers. To be a fisherman you have to be a kind of amateur —
JEAN.   Ichthyologist.
DAN.   Ichthyopsychologist. But what do I know. So, no sign. We row miles. Miles. *(Slowing down, tiring. Jean has sat down.)* You wouldn't believe the size of — there's one spot that's surrounded — both sides — with pines. Miles and miles, both sides. Anyway — *(Getting comfortable, against her, or on her lap. Jean continues to munch her sandwich.)* The sun goes down. No big deal.
JEAN.   No big deal.
DAN.   A little rose, a little amber. Nothing to notice. Basic everyday sundown. Then a bunch of disinterested strikes.
JEAN.   Uninterested.
DAN.   Uninterested strikes, all in a row. One two three four five six. So. There are fish in there; we just don't interest them much.
JEAN.   Is this the fish or is this the moon?
DAN.   Shhhh. This is the moon. This is the moon and the fish. This is both.... We're busy with the strikes; we don't even notice it's getting dark. Another couple of strikes, nibbles — bait stealings — nothing serious. And all of a sudden it's night. Pitch. Ink. We're two hours away, easily. Might as well turn around. So we start back — and ... up ... drifts ... this ... orange. Deep orange ... unstable ... major moon. *(Beat.)* The lake is like ...
JEAN.   Glass.
DAN.   ... Very calm. We're rowing back — it's just beautiful. It's important. We stopped rowing and watched it. And then I threw my line in — *(Simply.)* — just because we were stopping. And — "Galoompba." Immediately. *(Lying in her lap. Swaying with it.)* They swam up to that light like they were mesmerized by the light, dizzy on it ...
JEAN.   And that's when you caught them.
DAN.   All — however many of them. Five and seven.
JEAN.   Twelve.
DAN.   All twelve of them.
JEAN.   And by this time you were stoned.

DAN.  Uhhh.

JEAN.  Importantly stoned.

DAN.  Uhhh.

JEAN.  You bring back any grass?

DAN.  Of course not.

JEAN.  And what did you drink? *(Pause. Shakes him lightly.)* And what did you drink?

DAN.  We drank ... sunshine ... and moonshine ... and the air ... and trees ... and singing ... singing! And fish ... and camaraderie, and ... *(Mentally counts.)* Five six-packs.

JEAN.  You don't swim that well.

DAN.  Chad swims like a duck.

JEAN.  Ducks have rarely been known to save anyone from drowning more than once.

DAN.  This is true. I'm going to go to bed. *(Gets up.)* Give me a kiss. *(Kisses her lightly.)* I'm going to go to bed. *(Exits.)*

JEAN.  *(Pause.)* I don't think I've ever been more awake. *(Pause.)* There's an old Chinese proverb: If you save someone from drowning, you're responsible for them for the rest of their life. I think Dan feels it's the other way around.

DELIA.  I wasn't overly enthusiastic about the Orient.

JEAN.  I'd like to see India. Japan.

DELIA.  No, no ... I couldn't take the Indian deities with their fucking Mona Lisa smiles saying: "Well, that's for us to know and you to find out." I made the only rationalization possible. I decided they didn't know at all. Come drift with me on a raft in the sea of tranquillity. I'd go nuts. All of which would have served me very well if I could have forgotten it was a rationalization.

JEAN.  Don't you make yourself tired with all that?

DELIA.  *(Profound sigh; pause.)* Yes.

JEAN.  I mean, they're only pieces of sculpture. They're art objects. They're not Shiva and Shakti themselves. Shakti didn't come down and sit for her portrait. She didn't pose for the artist.

DELIA.  *(Beat.)* I believe she did. I think that she did. You're not easily quailed by the inscrutable.

JEAN.  Inscrutable. In. I-N, in. Scrut. S-C-R-U-T, scrut. Inscrut.

Ah. A, ah. Inscruta — ble. B-L-E, ble. Inscrutable. Inscrutable: I-N-S-C-R-U-T-A-B-L-E, inscrutable. *(Cynthia, in a robe, comes down, mildly surprised to see them. She hesitates only a second, then, without thinking further about it, crosses the room to the back door and lets herself out. They watch but do not comment.)*

DELIA. *(After a moment.)* Men. God, they're sad — depressing poor bastards, breaking their balls for their families. We're their reflection, I suppose, but I don't know as they love us for it. *(August enters, goes to the refrigerator, looks in.)* Who would have the time? I wonder, do we drive them to it?

JEAN. Women? *(August takes a bottle of milk from the refrigerator, sets it on a table, goes for a glass, leaving the refrigerator door open.)*

DELIA. No. Wives. I have an odd vision that women are wonderful. It's the wives. Sad old wives. *(August pours milk into the glass, and sits at the table staring off.)* I wouldn't be a man. Not and carry the dumbfounding load they've saddled themselves with. Actually, now that I think of it, being a woman is worse. We're the remains. We're what's left. We're the lees in the bottom of the bottle. You know how the world ends? You know what the "with a whimper" is? A sad old world of widows: wizened old women, lined up on beaches along all the Southern coastlines looking out over the water and trying to keep warm. *(Beat.)* Good Lord. That sounds so horribly right I'll bet it's prophetic. The species crawls up out of the warm ocean for a few million years and crawls back to it again to die. Why don't you make me a drink.

JEAN. No. *(August notices the light from the refrigerator, returns the bottle, closes the refrigerator door. Blackout. A flashlight beam moves slowly across the stage, investigating the chairs, the refrigerator, the floor. The light goes out. We hear the screen door creak and close. A pause.)*

## End of First Act

# ACT TWO

*Everyone except Kirsten is onstage, Dan presiding.*

DAN. Well, it's wrong is what it is. It's all wrong. Show her the Polaroid.

CYNTHIA. *(Handing Jean a print.)* You won't be able to tell much.

AUGUST. Burials have a way of turning up just as the light goes.

JEAN. I can't tell a thing from this.

DAN. *(Looking over her shoulder.)* See, he's laid out straight, head to the right.

JEAN. He isn't missing a hand, by any chance?

DAN. No, he's got the usual number of hands and three feet. Which is kinda funny when you see it.

CYNTHIA. Very awkward for dancing.

JEAN. Are you going to play with me, or are you going to tell me what you've found?

CYNTHIA. The third foot is incursive from some neighbor.

DAN. We don't know what we've found until we go over and see who his buddy is, and how many of them there are.

AUGUST. Tomorrow.

DAN. You're damn right.

CYNTHIA. Come out tomorrow, you might actually see August with a trowel in his hand.

DAN. Something's up; it's all wrong. Remember the round-house I showed you? With the fire in the middle? Well, these guys are buried under the roundhouse.

AUGUST. Looks almost as if the house was built over them.

JEAN. And that's not cricket.

DAN. Uh — no. That's not cricket.

JEAN. Does he have artifacts around him?

DAN. Very low caste. Not so much as a little stone pipe.

JEAN. You think they had a caste system?

CYNTHIA. All the latest advancements.

48

DAN.  As a matter of fact, around 1500 a tribe called the Natchez ended up down in Mississippi, where the French settlers studied them for about fifty years, decided they were dangerous, and rubbed them out —

JEAN.  — Oh, God —

DAN.  — Exactly. And it looks like the Natchez might have been the last of the Mound Builders. Hey, Deek — want to write a book? *Last of the Mound Builders* — I'd be glad to advise for a small consideration.

DELIA.  Delia or D.K. Not "Deek."

DAN.  So. If our guys were anything like the Natchez, they had a really off-the-wall, really bizarre, caste system.

AUGUST.  Four distinct castes:  The Suns —

DAN.  — who were the very big muck-a-mucks, led by the Great Sun, who was a God-King.

AUGUST.  Then the Nobles, then the Honored Men, and then the Stinkards.

DAN.  Really. Stinkards. Or that's the French translation. And of course most everybody was a Stinkard.

CYNTHIA.  So things haven't changed all that much.

AUGUST.  — and the Suns, the Nobles, and the Honored Men could only marry into the Stinkard class, with the second generation assuming the class of the mother. So only someone with a Sun mother and a Stinkard father could become the new God-King.

DAN.  And everybody married Stinkards. Including the other Stinkards.

CYNTHIA.  I didn't realize that.

AUGUST.  I thought probably you did.

DAN.  So they were an "upward-mobile," matriarchal society with a God-King muck-a-muck. All dressed in swan feathers. Carried on a litter everywhere he went. Like Delia; huh, D.K.?

DELIA.  Dan, it has been years since I've dressed in swan feathers.

JEAN.  How long did they live? Not the Natchez, our guys.

DAN.  Short.

JEAN.  How long? How short?

AUGUST.  If they reached the age of fifteen, their life expectancy was maybe thirty. *(A light thunder is heard, and gradually a wind rises.)*

DAN.  Do not ask how old I'll be my next birthday.

CYNTHIA.  You haven't reached the age of fifteen.

JEAN.  And won't. The head of the department calls him "Pollyandy" to his face.

AUGUST.  The head of the department is an extremely nihilistic individual.

DAN.  This is true.

JEAN.  What did they eat?

DAN.  *(Who has gone back to studying drawings of the grave site.)* Huh? Oh — corn, squash, beans —

CHAD.  That's succotash.

DAN.  You kill, right? When you can't flunk 'em? They ate everything. Shellfish, deer ...

CHAD.  For all you know, they were cannibals.

DAN.  Of course; you know, I'd love to discover they were cannibals. Only I doubt if we'd ever be funded again. They had fairly elaborate ritualistic human sacrifices, but they weren't barbarians.

CYNTHIA.  Actually, there's evidence that they did practice cannibalism.

DAN.  None. Here? None. You're talking about Wisconsin. The people of southern Illinois are certainly not responsible for the perverted table manners of the people of Wisconsin. I personally wouldn't be surprised at anything that was discovered in Wisconsin. I think there's something in the water that twists their minds.

CHAD.  Beer.

DAN.  Very likely. Exactly.

AUGUST.  Is that rain?

DAN.  Is it raining? Damn. I better go down and see that they got everything covered. *(Getting a slicker.)* Let up already. *(Going out.)* My God, it's pouring.

JEAN.  Put the hood up.

DAN.  *(Off.)* What?

JEAN.  Your hood, dummy. Put the hood up. *(Several slides of rain and the lake.)*

AUGUST. *(Isolated by the light to his desk area.)* Up, up, up, up. Every morning Dr. Loggins pushed a stake into the edge of the lake, trying, I think, to kill it. And every evening the lake had covered it. Nine tributaries empty into the basin, draining almost all of two counties. By the time the lake overran the site, it didn't at all matter. *(Chad knocks at the door. After a moment, Jean comes down.)*

CHAD.  I've been wanting to talk to you.

JEAN.  *(After an audible sigh.)* I think maybe if you didn't come here ... I mean, I know it's your house, and Dan likes you, you're a terrific relief from his gaggle of volunteers, but — you're putting yourself through something that seems so unnecessary.

CHAD.  I thought we should talk. Just with nobody —

JEAN.  We're talking, I don't mind; I'm perfectly willing to talk, but you can't expect it to be the sort of talk —

CHAD.  *(Overlapping from "expect," letting himself in.)* What? Are you trying to make a fool of me? We're not talking; I got my boat over here. We'll go over to the place, the six acres I told you about — it's gonna be an island when the lake fills, I want to show you. There's a cave. It's going to be under water in another couple of days ...

JEAN.  *(A long pause.)* No.

CHAD.  I thought you said we'd talk.

JEAN.  Say whatever it is you want to say. It won't improve with the change in scene.

CHAD.  It's just down at the landing —

JEAN.  You have some kind of romantic fantasy going on that frankly frightens —

CHAD.  I gave it a paint job; you ought to look at it.

JEAN.  Chad, for godsake, I don't even swim, I don't like water, I don't like boats, it's pouring rain, and I'm not at all attracted to you.

CHAD.  You don't know anything about me, you don't know —

JEAN.  That is absolutely true, but I can live with it. You said you wanted to talk; you don't want to talk, you want to bludgeon. I'm married to a guy you claim is your friend — I'm going — I'm very much committed to him — I'm really sorry, but you make me feel foolish.

CHAD. O.K., O.K., O.K., you don't want to be with just me. Maybe what you want is for the three of us to get together. Go out fishing ...

JEAN. *(Going.)* You're too much of a sport for me, Chad, you're too sporty for me.

CHAD. I thought you said we'd talk.

JEAN. Please put it out of your head, I don't like it. You make me uncomfortable.

CHAD. You said we'd talk. *(August enters with Kirsten.)* Bitch of a day, huh?

AUGUST. *(Shaking water from his hat.)* None too bright. *(Chad exits.)* I don't know, Jean — I think it's not a good idea to socialize too much with our little surrogate landlord.

JEAN. Socialize? — Dan seems to like him.

AUGUST. Well, Dan, for all his ebullience, is quite tactful really.

JEAN. And I'm not — or women aren't.

DAN. *(Entering soaked.)* Brother! Drowned.

JEAN. You really are. *(Hands Dan a towel.)* You get the girls into the motel?

DAN. Yeah, their tents were almost washing out from under them; they're game, but they're stupid. The lake is insane; it's ten feet higher than it's supposed to be — if it's raining tomorrow, we're going to have to work anyway.

JEAN. You get dried off?

DAN. Yeah, I'm fine.

KIRSTEN. *(At the table.)* What's in the sifter?

DAN. Seeds.

KIRSTEN. Maize? *(Pause.)* Maize?

DAN. Grass. *Cannabis sativa.*

KIRSTEN. Oh. *(Delia, dressed in a clean robe, walks unsteadily but unaided down the stairs.)*

DAN. Well. It walks, it talks. It takes nourishment from a spoon. *(August moves into the office.)*

DELIA. Spiritually it still crawls on its belly like a reptile. — And it no longer takes nourishment from a spoon.

JEAN.  You didn't.

DAN.  You know the Contemporary Lit. professor I told you about? Used to read your stuff out loud?

DELIA.  *(Sits.)* Don't push.

DAN.  Thought of his name. Dr. Landau. Had a great voice. Said — what do you think about this? — said —

DELIA.  I don't want to know what he said.

DAN.  No, you'll get a kick out of it.

JEAN.  This is about which one, this is *Spindrift?*

DAN.  Yeah, said you were checking off the possibilities of the species. You know, if it hadn't been for the —

DELIA.  That's such a load of crap, what a load of — you know what I wrote? How I teased myself through it? I set a simple problem and tried to solve it. Write a Chinese puzzle box. Write a Russian doll. A box within a box within a box within a box. Every time something was solved, within the solution was another problem, and within the solving of the second riddle another question arose. And when that riddle was unwound there was still a knot. And you know why I failed? For me? Because either a Chinese puzzle box must go on *ad infinitum* or there must finally be a last box. And when that box is opened, something must finally be in it. Something simple like maybe an answer. Or a fact, since we all seem to be compulsive compilers. Look at you, digging your evidence, piecing together shards, fragments, sherds. Clues, footnotes, artifacts, pollen grains, bones, chips.

DAN.  *(Overlapping from "pollen grains.")* Not of themselves — in association. Where are they, why are they there?

DELIA.  Boxes in boxes.

DAN.  *(Simultaneously overlapping second "boxes.")* Boxes in boxes. And when you got all the knots unwound in your book, and all the problems untied, and got down to the final little box —

DELIA.  The Russian doll.

DAN.  — and it was opened, what was inside?

DELIA.  *(Pause.)* Another book.

DAN.  *(Pause.)* I didn't know there was another ...

DELIA.  Well, that shows what you know. I thought it should

be for Dad. A simple ... simple.... Then, of course, Dad died, and I — *(Pause.)*

JEAN.    What?

DELIA.    "In Memoriam" never interested me much.

DAN.    *(Softly.)* There wasn't another ...

DELIA.    For you to see? For Dr. Landau to read aloud? I heard it — I saw it down there somewhere ... that graceful, trim, and dangerous leviathan that got away — it moved in the cold depths of some uncharted secret currents where the sun has never warmed the shadows. Graceful and taunting. Moving through a spectrum of dark colors alien to the un-aided eye. I could have captured it and displayed to the light some undiscovered color. But it was deaf to my charms and tokens and incantations. I called the son of a bitch, but it wouldn't rise. So I went down to find it.

DAN.    *(Pause.)* And it got away ...

DELIA.    *(Laughs.)* Well, I didn't get away. It caught me!

DAN.    Tell me about —

DELIA.    Tell me about the three-footed skeleton you've found.

DAN.    We can't work, Delia; how can we work in this? *(Goes to office door.)*

AUGUST.    If it's this bad tomorrow, we'll put up tarps.

JEAN.    I've thought about that house you grew up in. Big old masculine rooms with medical charts.

DELIA.    Oak floors and old oak furniture. And light. The whole place filled with sunlight. Especially in the winter.

AUGUST.    She left when she was seventeen; I'm surprised she'd tell anyone about it.

DELIA.    I'm the one who liked it, so I'm the one who re-members it.

AUGUST.    I never said I didn't like it.

DELIA.    He liked it so much he sold it the first week he could. Without mentioning to me that it was up for sale —

AUGUST.    You were being sick in Mexico, as I recall, and couldn't come to the funeral.

JEAN.    Boy, you two make me glad I'm an only child and grew up with grandparents.

AUGUST. It's all quite past. That's all past. Water under the bridge. Water under the bridge.

DAN. Water, water, water, water, water — *(Slide: bone awl.)*

AUGUST. This bone awl you might as well enter as made by one Mr. Cochise Mississippi, around A.D. 1100.

DAN. *(Overlapping.)* Mississippian; around A.D. 1100, give or take fifty years; it's made from a turkey metacarpal bone.

JEAN. You get into some far-afield studies, don't you?

DAN. Umm.

AUGUST. Most everything we're finding here is remarkably well preserved. *(Cynthia enters.)*

DELIA. *(Handing the bone awl to Jean.)* Well, that's a real keen bone awl, Cochise, but what have you done recently?

CYNTHIA. More recently they vanished without a trace. Along with the whole Mississippian Culture.

DELIA. Along with nearly everyone; vanished without a trace.

DAN. *(Still leaning against the screen, watching the rain.)* Vanished without a trace, vanished without a trace, vanished without a trace? God, I wish it would stop raining. Vanished without a trace. Nine mounds and a hothouse do not constitute without a trace. We've seen the outline of the foundations of houses used for gentlemen's clubs, complete with fireplace, never mind the ventilation. Vanished without a trace. It happens that this awl is one of the finest-crafted utilitarian tools discovered in North America — Cochise did not disappear without a trace. I think we have palpable evidence of his craft, of a subtle skill and imagination, of his care and conscientiousness. I think with his example his family stood proud and neat. I think his wife fashioned for him quilled buckskin aprons and kilts of surpassing brilliance that dazzled the tribe. Past? Vanished? Without a trace? Cochise? His passing, women, was mourned by tribes up and down the length of this river. I think his friends told histories around the fire of his craftiness in trapping game. Women cried and brave warriors walked out into the woods to be alone and fathom his loss. I think odes were composed and spoken and learned and repeated down the generations; songs were sung. I think so sure and strong a warrior stood as an example that young braves and children held up to themselves; I think Cochise was extraordinary beyond precedent. He danced with grace, he bathed twice a day, he spoke with simplicity and truth, and nursed the sick back to strength; he tamed wild animals and laughed when the children were frightened at night. I think he spread his arms out in an open field in the sun and yellow-green parakeets that he had tamed to sit on his hands came when he called them. I think wolves nuzzled his thighs and allowed him to walk in the wild as their comrade a thousand years before anyone named Francis walked in Assisi! Goddamn this rain! *(He grabs his slicker, kicks the screen door open, and charges out into the rain.)*

JEAN.    Put the hood up! *(Pause.)* I have a feeling he really believes that. If it weren't for August, nothing they write would ever get published.

CYNTHIA.    If it weren't for Dan, the work wouldn't get done in the first place.

DELIA.    Parakeets?

CYNTHIA.    Don't get him started. Parakeets were as common in Illinois as the sparrow is now.

JEAN.    They weren't tropical?

DELIA.    Some things we don't know, huh?

AUGUST.    We have no clear idea what the bone awl was actually used for, but it was undoubtedly used for something. This is a particularly good one. *(He goes into the office.)*

CYNTHIA.    Chad Jasker said he'd drive me into town; I think he's changed my plans.

JEAN.    He was —

DELIA.    I just left him standing on every corner; all the Mediterranean youths are hustlers.

CYNTHIA.    Hustlers? I don't know why you call him a hustler. The Mediterraneans are probably poor, and he's poor.

DELIA.    Not by their standards he isn't. Poor hustlers, rich hustlers —

CYNTHIA.    You talk about how rich they're going to be —

JEAN.    They are though —

CYNTHIA.    Oh, they are not.

JEAN.    No, really. When the lake comes in, God, they own

56

about a mile of the shoreline.

CYNTHIA.  Poor people don't become rich. It takes capital to develop a lakeshore — they're rich with fantasy. They'll sell for what they think is money and be ripped off. They're not going to be rich.

JEAN.  To hear him tell it, it's settled. You've heard about the Holiday Inn and all that ... the place is going to be a spa ... they're sitting right in the middle of it.

CYNTHIA.  I'm sure they'll borrow from the usurers and have the whole property extorted out from under them.

DELIA.  I was only thinking, there are those who hustle and those who don't.

CYNTHIA.  There are winners and losers, givers and takers; there's the quick and the dead; Chad tries to be among the quick. Sometimes it shows. What are you? Or do you know?

DELIA.  I'm a nomad.

CYNTHIA.  And you're happy with that?

DELIA.  Happy has nothing to do with it, Cynthia.

CYNTHIA.  Well, it sure as hell wouldn't seem to.

DELIA.  *(Pause. Friendly.)* If it applied, I could ask you the same thing: Are you happy with that? But it doesn't apply.

CYNTHIA.  *(Backing down.)* Forgive me for bringing it up. There are things I need that you perhaps don't.

DELIA.  We all need them. It's a question of what you're willing to pay.

CYNTHIA.  Well. You're willing to pay a good deal more than I am.

JEAN.  No. She isn't.

DELIA.  I'm used to shopping in bargain basements, peasant bazaars. You're paying the gold of the realm for bazaar merchandise.

CYNTHIA.  All that glitters ...

JEAN.  I don't believe that.

CYNTHIA.  *(Letting it pass.)* I thought you had given up on men. Wasn't there some woman sculptor or someone?

DELIA.  Good God, no. Never. I know — I should have. A long time ago; I just never got around to it. Isn't it pathetic, it's too late to change.

JEAN. I don't think I could get into it. *(They laugh.)* Is that funny? I guess it is. Wasn't there a story about you and some woman? About tearing up some bar?

DELIA. Which bar?

JEAN. In Spain or somewhere. Oh, no! You were fighting. You were arrested.

DELIA. Not in Spain; I'd still be there.

JEAN. Did you know you made all the newspapers?

DELIA. Of course I knew. Why do you think I did it?

CYNTHIA. They used to call us for comments; we hadn't heard from her in four years.

DELIA. Now no one has. That was Cannes, Nice ... along that winding, cliff-hanging — in a Mazerati. That was P.R. That wasn't me. A couple of times I allowed myself to cause a brawl or pass out in the middle of the ring because I knew it was good for the biographer. If there's such a thing as sin any more, that must be high on the list. Which of the commandments would that come under? It's not really so bad to lie; sometimes it's kinder. Go ahead and steal, really, most of the bastards deserve to lose it. But I've "sinned." I've humiliated myself because people expected it of me.

CYNTHIA. *(Closing the refrigerator in disgust.)* Christ, this house is crammed with drugs. Doesn't anybody drink any more? *(Blackout.)*

AUGUST. Dianne, would you just note marginally that I have decided I am definitely sick of aesthetics. Aesthetics and all the representatives of the humanities ransacking anthropological collections for pots they find pleasingly shaped and carrying them off to museums, where they lecture without content on form — and without the least ethnological information or understanding. Aesthetics is becoming an enemy to thought. *(Pause. Slide: college graduation.)* What the hell is — Christ, this is my graduation — notice the innocent and hopeful countenance. Prepared to conquer lost worlds with a doctorate in one hand and a trowel in the other. *(Slide: Dan — a pause.)* A man's life work is taken up, undertaken, I have no doubt, to blind him to the passing moon. I have no doubt that in an area of his almost unconscious he knows this and therefore is not blinded but only driven. The dig at Jasker's Field was unfinished. A salvage operation from which we salvaged nothing. Slides of picnics, slides of houses, slides of water, slides of ducks, slides of boats, slides of pain, slides of need, slides of spear points. A great amount of work has been done on the early cultures of North America and we have found only the periphery of the culture. Three hundred mounds, numberless graves have been opened, usually seconds before the builders plowed them under. And of the Mississippian Culture — never before had the grave of a God-King been discovered. The most important find in forty years of work. We do not allow ourselves to dream of finding what we might find and dream with every sweep of a trowel. And what is salvaged? Nothing. Nothing. *(To the slides.)* Nothing. Nothing. Nothing. Nothing. Nothing. Nothing. *(Jean and Delia are reading. There are approaching sounds of girls yelling, everyone yelling, Dan's voice heard approaching. They stand as he enters. The slides continue flicking repeatedly across the screen.)*

DAN.   Jean, Jean, Jean, Jean — come out — come down — the muck-a-muck. The high and holy muck-a-muck —

JEAN.   — What? Who is it? In the grave? —

DAN.   Not one — I'll be very calm, I'm not trembling, shit, I'm fine — We started clearing away toward the third foot — you remember the — grave, the —

JEAN.   — Sure, sure.... The Stinkard —

DAN.   — Third foot? He isn't a Stinkard, he's a retainer, dozens of them — all over the place — and in the center the ground is dark — a big black square where there has been a log tomb. It's all rotted away, but the ground is dark. August said, Oh, my God. Oh, my God. It's the tomb of a God-King. Nobody's ever found — *(Breathes deeply.)* You have never seen anything like it. Never. We didn't know if they had gold — but a gold thing on his face — and copper — Beautiful copper breastplates — everywhere — pearls like — obsidian axes, beads, thousands of tons of — come on. Delia, if you don't come out and see this, I'll never read another word you — I swear to you, two more days and the lake would have flooded it. We're going to have to break our asses.

JEAN.  A muck-a-muck? A God-King?

DAN.    Oh, God, what a god he must have been! Pottery. *Glazed* pots — fifty, sixty of them. It's going to be dark in no time; hurry up, it's soaking wet — we're up to our knees — Oh, my God, how famous we're going to be! You gotta write the book, Delia, you really gotta write it.

DELIA.    I'll come down and see. If I can't make it, I expect to be carried on the muck-a-muck's litter.

DAN.    I'll carry you on my back.

JEAN.    Pearls?

DAN.    A room full — and maybe *gold.* This mask thing. We thought they might have gold. They had trade routes into country where there's gold. Copper armbands, bracelets. I am perfectly calm. I am a mature and balanced scientist. I wish you could see August up to his ass in mud. He said, "This is a very high muck-a-muck." *(Delia and Jean hurry off.)* What am I supposed to get? I was supposed to get something. *(August, Chad, Cynthia, Jean, Delia, and Kirsten, all carrying boxes, overrun him, pass back and forth, busy with things, working, tired and high, but preoccupied. Kirsten goes upstairs.)*

CYNTHIA.    Pitch black, it's absolutely maddening. You know you're not going to keep it under your hat.

AUGUST.    For a while; for a day.

CYNTHIA.    *(To Chad.)* You're pledged, you know that — not a word. Because if it gets out, it's all over; we'll have to set up guards.

CHAD.    You could get lights, you could work at night —

AUGUST.    That would be subtle.

DAN.    We'd draw a larger crowd than the World Series.

AUGUST.    You called Croff?

CYNTHIA.    Yes, again. You want to know what he said again? *(They go back to working — she tells the women.)* He pissed. He was absolutely wetting his pants. He kept saying, Where's August? I said, he's down at the goddamned dig, where would you be? He started looking up charter-plane companies. I said, Croff, don't sweat it, we won't be doing anything until it gets light; drive down in the morning. He's already calculating the size of the grant the college will be getting from this. He has

60

his picture on the cover of *Newsweek*. He honest-to-God asked me when *Scientific American* went to press.

DAN. Jasker's the one who's going to be famous, you know that, don't you? *(As the work organizes itself, Dan is painting green copper beads with nail polish; August is cleaning something as delicately as an artist; Cynthia is writing the location and date numbers on projectile points, pottery shards, and small envelopes of pearls; Jean is entering the numbers on a chart.)*

CYNTHIA. It's going to be the most important archaeological dig in America.

DAN. Well, north of the Rio.

CHAD. You know, no bull, I admire you people. You're really trying to make something of yourself. You could have been on vacation like everybody else. I'd just make a bet — you're not doing it for what you get. I've watched you down there and I wouldn't have the patience for it.

CYNTHIA. They wouldn't have the patience to bust down a transmission or any of the tinkerings that —

CHAD. — No, you do that 'cause you got to do it; 'cause you'd be embarrassed not to. But, see — you guys are finding little pieces of charcoal last week and stuff if I saw on the ground I wouldn't bother to bend down for, but now that you found something — what's something in that grave that's valuable? I mean, that you could sell?

CYNTHIA. Almost everything.

DAN. — No more hitches with funding, you realize that. We'll be turning people down.

AUGUST. Well, now, no point in being high-handed.

CHAD. If someone came along and offered you — where's the thing? The gold thing? The bead?

DAN. Jean?

JEAN. On the table.

CHAD. See? Sitting on the table. If someone offered to buy this —

AUGUST. Very carefully, Mr. Jasker. That's the first gold ever —

CHAD. I know, I watched you with it. How much would you ask for that, how much is that worth?

AUGUST. *(Carefully.)* The gold in it — is worth maybe two or three dollars. It's beaten very thin and spread around a wooden bead. The wood has long since disintegrated. *(Taking it.)* You can hear it rattle inside. You felt how light it was.

CHAD. See, two dollars. You'd only ask what it was really worth — you wouldn't try to make anything for — Like what you really want to know is — aw, no — well —

AUGUST. I suppose if we knew that —

CHAD. *(Over.)* No, forget I said it, I can't say it; I'm not saying it right; I don't know what I'm trying to say. What are these?

AUGUST. *(Taking them from him.)* Why do you come here?

CHAD. *(Beat.)* Beg pardon, Doc? Whatta you mean?

AUGUST. You could be any number of places.

CYNTHIA. We undoubtedly have our attractions, August.

AUGUST. You were down at the dig last week watching the excavation of a fire pit. Charcoal and split rocks. Anyone could see there was no intrinsic material value in that find.

CHAD. Yeah, I know, but it's —

AUGUST. You asked when it had been built, how old it was — which were the precise questions we were asking ourselves.

CHAD. No, I'm not putting it right.

AUGUST. People are drawn to speculate. Even my sister, who has no curiosity about anything —

DAN. I'm going to get her to write us up, though. Fictionalized, of course.

AUGUST. I think archaeology can survive without that.

CHAD. Now you got your boss impressed; he's going to be down —

DAN. Something like this, we need people to verify that we aren't faking it — it's —

AUGUST. *(Minimizing.)* He's the sort that likes to check up on his employees. He's come down a number of times. Generally unannounced.

CHAD. I gotta have another beer. See, that's why I come here; I can always count on Dan to turn me on.

CYNTHIA. Oh, I think you can be turned on by any number of things.

AUGUST. *(He lifts from the table the fragile gold mask he has been cleaning.)* Look at this, coming out beautifully.

CYNTHIA. *(Getting her camera and a flash unit.)* I want to get this.

DAN. It's a death mask — we guess. It might have had feathers around it here. We have to guess. We've never seen anything like it before. *(He holds it up to his face, and almost inadvertently it stays in place.)* Is that incredible? Tell me I look like a God-King.

JEAN. Don't put that —

DAN. I didn't do a thing.

CYNTHIA. Smile. Or can you? *(Flash.)*

DAN. Let me see. I'm blind. Help me with it. *(August carefully lifts it from Dan's face.)* That's the same design we've seen on gorgets, and assumed it was meant to represent pigmentation.

CHAD. That thing's solid gold, isn't it?

AUGUST. *(A lie.)* That's copper — they valued it above gold.

DAN. It's fragile as hell. He didn't wear it, you know — they made it for him after he died. If you can imagine it completely surrounded with feathers.

JEAN. I really didn't like it on you at all.

DAN. Are you crazy; every dead God-King is wearing one this year. It may take a while to catch on.

CHAD. These are beads; they're copper too?

DAN. Those will fall right apart, Chad, they're corroded right through. They're made the same as the gold — they beat out a solid nugget of copper — they had no metallurgical knowledge, to speak of.

CYNTHIA. What have you got all over your hands?

CHAD. Oh, that's uh — paint; got more on me than I did on the car.

CYNTHIA. You painted your car?

DELIA. It's a different car.

CHAD. Got a new one; painted it black. I had 'em put on the papers that it was black, it was some kind of green, all rusted off; I had to paint it before I got stopped.

CYNTHIA.   You sold the blue one?

CHAD.   Wrapped it up.

CYNTHIA.   The Olds?

CHAD.   Couple a days ago, over on 14.

DAN.   He wraps it around a tree, gets out, leaves it there, and hitches a lift home.

CHAD.   Sheriff comes by, says they towed it to the dump, tried to give me a summons for abandoning it. I told him I was dazed; I didn't know what I was doing ...

DAN.   How'd you know it was a different car?

DELIA.   I'm familiar with all possible transportation in and out of here.

JEAN.   What's that stuff you're putting on that?

DAN.   Just nail polish, help hold it together.

JEAN.   Smells vile.

DAN.   You look tired; don't get sick again.

CHAD.   You been sick?

JEAN.   No. Woozy; tired, not sick.

DAN.   I think she's developing evening sickness. You've heard of morning sickness; she's getting evening sickness.

JEAN.   *(To Cynthia.)* Did you have that?

CYNTHIA.   Boring as hell, isn't it?

CHAD.   What from?

DAN.   Who knows the metabolism of a pregnant woman? She'll feel better tomorrow; she can diagnose what was wrong with her and write a paper on it.

JEAN.   Might do it too.

CHAD.   Since when was you — *(A long pause. His face registers the implication of the statement. They do not notice and continue working.)*

AUGUST.   *( To Dan.)* What are you hiding there? *(Dan gives him a box, which August begins to sort through.)*

CHAD.   *(Finally. Pinched.)* When's it due?

DAN.   December, January.

CHAD.   Hell, probably ought to celebrate.

DAN.   Thought I told you.

CHAD.   Not me.

DAN.   As big as the hole is in the gold bead, what would

you think — these are all small — if several ropes of copper beads came down like this and then the strings went through the gold one.

AUGUST. Where's the Polaroid of his chest; how was the copper situated?

CYNTHIA. *(Overlapping Dan from "gold bead.")* What did you say you were going to show me on your car?

CHAD. Me?

CYNTHIA. I don't know; you said you had something in the trunk.

CHAD. Trunk's locked. I don't have the key for it.

CYNTHIA. Maybe it was the hood, I don't know.

CHAD. I think you're thinking of someone else.

CYNTHIA. *(Going out the door.)* Well, anyway, I want to see this famous paint job.

CHAD. I ain't got time. I gotta get going. *(Savage whisper.)* Leave me alone.

CYNTHIA. *(Goes to the refrigerator, gets out a beer.)* Anyone else? Auggie?

AUGUST. I'm fine.

CHAD. *(Finally. Hardly audible, but hard.)* Whatta you gonna call it? *(As Jean, who has heard, starts to leave.)* HEY! *(Everyone freezes.)* Said, what name you gonna name it?

DAN. What?

CHAD. *(Almost in tears.)* The baby.

DAN. We're taking all suggestions, putting them in a hat.

CHAD. What then, you'll pull it out like a rabbit? It's no more important to you than that?

DAN. Well, we figure when we have a palpable, honest-to-God kid, with a gender, we'll think of something. *(Kirsten comes down, hangs back at the stairs.)*

CHAD. Boy, you guys are supercool, supercool. Down here in the sticks, you got your little harem of ugly girl students around you watching every little brush stroke and pick and pry like you was painting the world's last masterpiece. You got your pretty wives and your kids and your drug-addict sister. You really got everything going for you. Cynthia says you're going to be getting write-ups in *Time* magazine.

CYNTHIA. I said Croff envisions his mug on the cover.

CHAD. You got the place all tied up so anything you find belongs to you. You're really knocking it.

AUGUST. That was the agreement your father signed.

CHAD. *(Not hearing.)* I really got to admire your supercool.

DAN. We got it knocked.

CHAD. You really got it knocked. You're digging up all these old battle weapons — *(Lifting from the box a foot-long spear point.)* Just look at the craftsmanship on that — what'd you say that was? You called that a spear point. Who'd think those old boys would have the tools to make something like that.

AUGUST. That's very dangerous.

CYNTHIA. You said you had to be somewhere by —

CHAD. Hell, you don't even need — you can break someone's neck just by putting the right twist in the right place. *(He has, as quick as a snake, reached around Cynthia's neck with his arm.)* You know that?

CYNTHIA. I'm sure you could. You're a lot stronger than I. *(He releases her.)*

CHAD. It's a damn shame you're going to have to find yourself some other field of operation.

DAN. We'll be a while on this one yet.

CHAD. I'm talking about next year.

DAN. Next year we can get back to those mounds you think are so important.

CHAD. I guess you can if you can find where the road-construction crew scatters them. Only I don't think the Holiday Inn people are going to much appreciate a scruffy gang of ugly virgins digging up the front yard of their motel.

CYNTHIA. I don't know why you think they're virgins.

DAN. People eating at your restaurant?

CHAD. You think it's cute? You think it's not going to happen? There are some cost accountants and some professional architects from down at Memphis you should talk to.

DAN. The tourists are going to be flooding the place heavier than the lake, huh?

CHAD. You may know a hell of a lot about your grave robbing but you're really full of shit when it comes to commerce.

I know you've had your nose stuck in the ground; it's not easy to see what's going on around you from that position, but this is the last trip you fellows are making down here —

DAN.   — You don't seem to realize the importance of what's happened here today. Coordinating this site with the information we're going to be getting from the mounds — The information we have already will take years —

CHAD.   *(Overlapping from "we have.")* You're just going to have to go on what you've got, buddy.

DAN.   — It's a man's life work here —

CHAD.   'Cause as it happens, I don't want you here. And there ain't going to be any mounds. The mounds are going to be fucking flat. The mounds are going to be under about forty tons of highway interchange. They're going to be under a tennis court.

DAN.   I mean, it doesn't matter whether you understand or not, but I'd think you'd want to be part of that. Goddamn! If you want tourists coming in here, we're going to have to be digging around them.

DAN.   I don't want to hear about your tennis courts.

CHAD.   You people are dreaming! You might not like it, but there ain't no mounds next year. There's an interchange coming through you maybe don't know about.

DAN.   I know all about it; the site is archaeologically too important to be superseded by —

CHAD.   *(Overlapping from "to be superseded.")* They may be hot shit to you; Dad and me don't happen to want our property —

DAN.   You don't realize how important a man like August Howe is. Jesus Christ, you talk like —

CHAD.   — My land, baby! MY LAND! MY LAND! It don't belong to your Indian god. It don't belong to you. It's my land and there is an Interstate coming through. Now, if you want to sit in its way, every one of you, good, you're invited.

KIRSTEN.   The Interstate isn't coming through your land.

AUGUST.   That isn't necessary now.

CHAD.   Hell, it isn't. You think they're going to build a motel where there isn't a highway?

DAN. *(Overlapping from "where there.")* Then they won't build it. What the hell difference does it make? You're talking about a goddamn Holiday Inn.

CHAD. They been here! I've seen the plans!

DAN. Goddamnit, there's a law since 1954 — in this state — against public-funded construction defacing Indian monuments.

CHAD. *(Beat.)* Well, guys, I hate to disappoint you, but you're thinking about it a little late.

DAN. We thought about it two years ago. *(Pause.)* When did you last hear from your motel architects?

CHAD. What do you mean, two years ago?

DAN. Professor Howe prepared a —

AUGUST. — Not tonight. In the morning —

DAN. *(Right over.)* — August prepared a report to the legislature on the importance of this site —

CHAD. — Well, I'm sorry he went to all the trouble —

DAN. The highway isn't going to be anywhere near Blue Shoals. It's been rerouted to the other side of the goddamn lake! We got notice before we came down this summer. *(A long pause.)*

CYNTHIA. When was this, August?

CHAD. Shit. "When" — Let on like —

DAN. Two years; after our first summer; after we heard about the highway.

CYNTHIA. It must have been a lot of trouble keeping me in the dark.

DELIA. We're a bad risk, Cynthia.

AUGUST. It was a matter of a brief report, a few pictures, and a phone call.

JEAN. You can't do that.

DAN. Old man Jasker wouldn't allow the land to become a national monument. How else could we protect them?

CYNTHIA. Them? Protect them or protect you?

CHAD. Boy, you're pretending to be my friend; you're listening to me talking about soul food and grilled bass out of the lake; what are you saying behind my back? Leading me on. Where do you get off thinking you're better than the people around here and can take over and take away everything we hope for — where — laughing about my goddamned island — what do you care. Millions! You're trying to steal from me!

JEAN.   You don't know what it means to him.

DAN.   I know what it means to me; you should know what it means to me.

CYNTHIA.   Using my photographs of the dig to surreptitiously —

DAN.   Chad, I'm trying to make you see that you'd be better off — understand the value of what you have here, God, the place —

CHAD.   *(A howling scream.)* NOOOOOOOOO! *(Silence. A pained plea.)* How can you treat people...? *(Pause.)*

JEAN.   Chad. I went down to the courthouse; I saw the model you told me to see, I ...

CHAD.   *(Fiercely to August.)* — you won't get it. I know what you want, Professor, but you might just have to stay up at State next summer with your whore and fuck her yourself. *(He exits.)*

CYNTHIA.   Chad? *(Going out.)* Jasker, goddamnit, stay here. Talk to me! I didn't know.

DAN.   What model at the courthouse?

JEAN.   Of the motel and the resort; it isn't important.

DELIA.   I may take you up, Dan, on writing that book.

AUGUST.   I'm glad you're walking; I don't think it's necessary for you to stay.

DELIA.   Not at all. Cynthia said Jasker'd be ripped off — I guess —

AUGUST.   If I thought it were possible for you to write, I'd admonish against it.

DELIA.   You always have. I never needed either your approval or "admonishments"; Dad respected what I was doing, that was enough for me.

AUGUST.   What you never realized was that Dad and I were close. You didn't want us to be, so you supposed it to be the way you wanted.

DELIA.   *(Overlapping on "you supposed.")* — I was never interested in your opinion of anything I was —

AUGUST.  — Thinking you were some kind of *wunderkind* and assuming —

DELIA.  — He respected what I was doing and that was —

AUGUST.  — Dad never read a word you wrote. He quoted your reviews back to you verbatim and laughed behind your back because you never noticed. He thought you were a fool.

CYNTHIA.  *(Re-enters, goes upstairs.)* Come upstairs, Kirsten; come to bed.

AUGUST.  Dan, it's late, I hadn't thought we'd sleep much tonight, but maybe that's the best thing to do. We'll be getting up at five. *(Leaving.)*

DELIA.  Dad's opinion was always too important to me. Thank you.

AUGUST.  You're welcome. *(He is gone, so is Delia; the others begin to leave as the night sounds increase, along with a weirdly close screech owl, and the lights fade as tractor sounds are heard. As the stage becomes dark, we can hear someone moving about.)*

DAN'S VOICE.  Hello? Jesus Christ. Is somebody down there? *(Pause. Flashlight.)* Delia? Hello? *(The beam catches Chad full in the face. He is wearing the God-King's mask, and has the knapsack in his arms. He stands perfectly still.)*

CHAD.  The light's in my face.

DAN.  *(The beam from the flashlight moves to Chad's loaded arms. Dan stays on the stairs.)* Chad?

CHAD.  Cynthia said you was a light sleeper. *(Pause.)*

DAN.  Yeah.

CHAD.  I got something I want to show you. *(Pause.)*

DAN.  You … shouldn't handle … *(Pause.)*

CHAD.  It's only copper. They treasured it higher than gold.

DAN.  What have you got in — what are you doing?

CHAD.  There's something outside I want to show you.

DAN.  What?

CHAD.  Come outside. *(He moves to the door.)*

DAN.  Don't go out with that …

CHAD.  There's something I want to show you.

DAN.  Chad? *(The light plays across the empty table.)* Chad? *(Back to the door through which Chad has disappeared outside.)*

CHAD. *(Off.)* I want to show you something. *(Dan moves down the stairs and out. As a slow dawn begins, a girl's voice is heard calling, "Dr. Loggins?" repeatedly, then another girl calling the same. August, barely awake, stumbles down, buckling his belt, yells out the window, "Yes, goddamnit," and goes off. Kirsten follows him almost immediately, but stops at the bottom of the stairs as Delia, fully dressed, enters.)*

KIRSTEN. *(Sullen.)* Good morning.

DELIA. Good morning. *(Kirsten goes out as Delia takes a bottle of tonic from the refrigerator.)*

JEAN. *(Entering.)* My God, real clothes.

DELIA. The better to leave your enclave. *(The light continues to intensify.)*

JEAN. Oh. Well, I guess you know what you need. Did Pollyandy sleep down here last night or did he even get home?

DELIA. I don't know.

JEAN. I woke up; then I managed to get pissed off enough to go back to sleep. He said something about celebrating the God-King's discovery with a mescaline trip, but I think he was blithering.

DELIA. Where would anyone get mescaline in Blue Shoals, Illinois?

JEAN. You've been away longer than you know. *(Going out.)* It's gorgeous out. *(There are a few noises, girls' voices, August's.)*

CYNTHIA. *(Off.)* What? *(Muffled answer.)* I'll be down — Said, I'll be down. *(She appears.)* The son of a bitch. I'll kill him.

DELIA. You'll kill whom?

AUGUST. *(Off.)* It's mad — He's a madman, it's crazy —

JEAN. *(Off.)* August, where is —

AUGUST. *(Entering.)* Not now, damnit; not now.

CYNTHIA. Chad Jasker.

AUGUST. Everything's gone. He's carried everything off — the bulldozer's been run over the site — the bulldozer is out in the lake in six feet of water, apparently where it got stuck — *(Cynthia goes out.)*

DELIA. Is Dan out there?

AUGUST. What's to do? There's nothing to do. Let him sleep it off.

KIRSTEN. *(Entering.)* The girls are calling you.

DELIA. *(As Jean enters.)* Jean, you'd better go in and call the county sheriff.

JEAN. Tell him he's wrecked the site.

DELIA. Tell him Dan is missing. *(Jean stands transfixed for a second. Turns and goes into the office.)*

AUGUST. Oh, God, no.

CYNTHIA. *(Entering.)* I tried to tell August he didn't know what he was dealing with.

AUGUST. Cynthia — I want you to sit down. *(Takes her hands.)*

CYNTHIA. What? *(Breaks away.)* Oh, please.

AUGUST. Please.

CYNTHIA. What? What is it? Don't hold on to me, you know I don't like to be grabbed at. What on earth ... *(Freeze. Looks around.)* He's left. He's run off ...

AUGUST. No, no, no, no ...

CYNTHIA. Where?

AUGUST. There's the possibility that —

CYNTHIA. Oh, damn your possibilities —

AUGUST. Dan hasn't — Dan isn't here. Did you talk to Jasker last night?

DELIA. Did he tell you anything?

CYNTHIA. I couldn't find him.

DELIA. What is Jasker capable of? I never looked at him twice until last night.

CYNTHIA. He'd do anything.

DELIA. You know what I'm talking about; I want to know if the madman is capable —

CYNTHIA. — Yes, yes! He's capable of anything —

DELIA. He hurt you; you know.

CYNTHIA. — Yes, repeatedly. Yes. *(Delia exits. Pause.)* You didn't tell me about the highway because you knew I'd tell him. I would have.

AUGUST. What matters is finding Dan.

CYNTHIA. We have nothing to show for our dig, August. We have nine pictures I took last night.

AUGUST. I know.

CYNTHIA. The little bastard thought he wiped us out completely, but we fooled him.

AUGUST. That isn't important to me.

CYNTHIA. What a stupid thing to lie about. *(As August starts to move away.)* Well, I can do one thing for him. *(Takes up the camera, ejects the film, and begins unrolling it.)*

AUGUST. Stop it! CYNTHIA!

CYNTHIA. *(Throwing the unrolled film on the floor as he reaches her.)* There! I can do that much for him. There's your dig.

JEAN. *(Entering.)* There are two police cars turning into the field if you want to go out. I'm trying to think where they might have ... *(The light immediately confines August to his desk area.)*

AUGUST. At eleven that morning an oar from Chad Jasker's boat was found floating near the center of the lake. At nine that night townspeople turned their car headlights out across the water to assist the divers who had come down from Marion. *(Car headlights swing across the room. Delia turns on a lamp.)*

JEAN. Where the hell are all the people coming from? Why don't they stay away?

CYNTHIA. People from town, volunteers; there's almost no police force.

KIRSTEN. They've got men with diving equipment.

JEAN. I can't help; I can't go outside; I'm swamped with commiserations. Keep those damn girls out of here; keep them all out.

CYNTHIA. August does that. They know better than to come here.

DELIA. Who's the old man?

CYNTHIA. Old man Jasker.

DELIA. What are all the goddamned people doing here; the cars keep turning into the area, there must be fifty cars.

CYNTHIA. They see the lights, they think we've discovered something.

DELIA. Can't they keep them away?

CYNTHIA. There's no law.

DELIA. All the laws are the wrong goddamned laws.

CYNTHIA.   Someone heard we had discovered a monster in the lake. The sightseers will go away; the men will work all night.

KIRSTEN.   They've got a lot of machinery for a small town.

JEAN.   *(Running to the screen door.)* THEY ARE NOT TO DRAG THE LAKE. THEY USE GRAPPLING HOOKS TO DRAG THE LAKE, THEY ARE NOT TO DRAG THE LAKE! They said they'd send for divers!

DELIA.   Shut up!

JEAN.   I'm going to be fine.

DELIA.   You can't help. Shut up.

JEAN.   Why did he go out? Why didn't someone hear him? Why did the girls stay at the motel? WHY DID HE HAVE TO HEAR NOISES IN THE NIGHT? WHY DID HE TRUST PEOPLE, WHY DID HE BELIEVE IN THINGS? *(Delia slaps her across the face. Holds her a moment. Jean sits. Delia sits beside her.)* Morbid, morbid, stupid people. Vanished without a trace. I'm going to be fine. Cochise. Co-C-O-co. Vanished without a trace. I want the bone awl. I want the —

CYNTHIA.   *(Going to her.)* Jean, please. Please. We don't have it. It's gone.

AUGUST.   Dianne, Dianne.... We left the house for the last time August 8. I went back in January, only hoping to see the lake take it away. In my mind's eye the river's currents swept the house before it as a great brown flood bears off everything in its path. That was in my mind's eye. The lake had risen to half-cover the house. Much of the second level was above the water. The house looked more scuttled than inundated. The lake rises as a great long hand-shaped pond, slowly ... *(Stops, turns the machine off. The women hardly move. Cynthia stares off, Jean sits, her head in Delia's lap.)*

CYNTHIA.   August won't work without Dan.

JEAN.   Does it matter?

CYNTHIA.   No.

DELIA.   Yes. Of course it does.

CYNTHIA.   He doesn't know he won't work.

DELIA.   Yes, he does.

JEAN.   *(Not moving.)* I'm too heavy on you.

DELIA. You weigh nothing.

JEAN. Are they gone?

DELIA. The divers will be back at nine.

CYNTHIA. They won't find them.

DELIA. Shhhh.

CYNTHIA. They won't find them.

DELIA. Shhhh.

CYNTHIA. They won't.

DELIA. Shhhh.

CYNTHIA. They won't find them. *(August presses the tape recorder. It plays.)*

AUGUST'S VOICE. *(On tape.)* … to see the lake take it away. In my mind's eye the river's currents swept the house before it as a great brown flood bears off everything in its path. That was in my mind's eye. The lake had risen to half-cover the house. Much of the second level was above the water. The house looked more scuttled than inundated. The lake rises as a great long hand-shaped pond, slowly … *(He turns the machine off a second, then turns it on.)*

AUGUST. Dianne … *(Turns machine off. After a moment he turns it on.)* Dianne … *(The women fade. August tries to frame a statement. The machine continues to record the stillness. August stands with the mike in his hand, very still. The tape continues to turn. A long pause. The lights fade on him.)*

**CURTAIN**

# PROPERTY LIST

Small tape recorder with microphone (AUGUST)
Luggage (DAN, CHAD, JEAN)
Suitcases, knapsacks (JEAN, CYNTHIA, KIRSTEN)
Flashlight (DAN)
Carton of cigarettes (CYNTHIA)
Matches or lighter
Medicine (CHAD)
Papers (CHAD)
Glass of wine (CYNTHIA)
Joints, to be rolled (DAN)
Purse (CYNTHIA)
Beer (DAN, CYNTHIA)
4 typed pages (DAN)
Dig equipment (CYNTHIA)
Fishing equipment: rod, reels, creels, etc. (CHAD, DAN)
Bottle of Scotch (CHAD)
Drinking glass (AUGUST)
Polaroid print (CYNTHIA)
Drawing of grave site (DAN)
Rain slicker (DAN)
Hat (AUGUST)
Towel (JEAN)
Bone awl (DELIA)
Reading matter (JAN, DELIA)
Boxes (CHAD, CYNTHIA, JEAN, DELIA, KIRSTEN)
Green copper beads, some with nail polish (DAN)
Dig finds: projectile points, shards, pearls (in envelope)
        (CYNTHIA)
Chart (JEAN)
Gold bead (CHAD)
Fragile gold mast (AUGUST)
Camera with flash unit (CYNTHIA)

Copper beads (CHAD)
Box (DAN)
Foot-long spear point (CHAD)
Bottle of tonic (DELIA)
Camera (CYNTHIA)
Roll of film (CYNTHIA)

# SOUND EFFECTS

Car stopping
Car doors slamming
Light thunder with gradually rising wind
Bulldozer
Night sounds

# NEW PLAYS

• **A QUESTION OF MERCY by David Rabe.** The Obie Award-winning playwright probes the sensitive and controversial issue of doctor-assisted suicide in the age of AIDS in this poignant drama. *"There are many devastating ironies in Mr. Rabe's beautifully considered, piercingly clear-eyed work ... " –The NY Times. "With unsettling candor and disturbing insight, the play arouses pity and understanding of a troubling subject ... Rabe's provocative tale is an affirmation of dignity that rings clear and true." –Variety.* [6M, 1W] ISBN: 0-8222-1643-4

• **A DOLL'S HOUSE by Henrik Ibsen, adapted by Frank McGuinness. Winner of the 1997 Tony Award for best revival.** *"New, raw, gut-twisting and gripping. Easily the hottest drama this season." –USA Today. "Bold, brilliant and alive." –The Wall Street Journal. "A thunderclap of an evening that takes your breath away." –Time. "The stuff of Broadway legend." –Associated Press.* [4M, 4W, 2 boys] ISBN: 0-8222-1636-1

• **THE WAITING ROOM by Lisa Loomer.** Three women from different centuries meet in a doctor's waiting room in this dark comedy about the timeless quest for beauty -- and its cost. *" ... THE WAITING ROOM ... is a bold, risky melange of conflicting elements that is ... terrifically moving ... There's no resisting the fierce emotional pull of the play." – The NY Times. " ... one of the high points of this year's Off-Broadway season ... THE WAITING ROOM is well worth a visit." –Back Stage.* [7M, 4W, flexible casting] ISBN: 0-8222-1594-2

• **MR. PETERS' CONNECTIONS by Arthur Miller.** Mr. Miller describes the protagonist as existing in a dream-like state when the mind is "freed to roam from real memories to conjectures, from trivialities to tragic insights, from terror of death to glorying in one's being alive." With this memory play, the Tony Award and Pulitzer Prize-winner reaffirms his stature as the world's foremost dramatist. *" ... a cross between Joycean stream-of-consciousness and Strindberg's dream plays, sweetened with a dose of William Saroyan's philosophical whimsy ... CONNECTIONS is most intriguing ... Miller scholars will surely find many connections of their own to make between this work and the author's earlier plays." –The NY Times.* [5M, 3W] ISBN: 0-8222-1687-6

• **THE STEWARD OF CHRISTENDOM by Sebastian Barry.** A freely imagined portrait of the author's great-grandfather, the last Chief Superintendent of the Dublin Metropolitan Police. *"MAGNIFICENT ... the cool, elegiac eye of James Joyce's THE DEAD; the bleak absurdity of Samuel Beckett's lost, primal characters; the cosmic anger of KING LEAR ..." –The NY Times. "Sebastian Barry's compassionate imaging of an ancestor he never knew is among the most poignant onstage displays of humanity in recent memory." –Variety.* [5M, 4W] ISBN: 0-8222-1609-4

• **SYMPATHETIC MAGIC by Lanford Wilson. Winner of the 1997 Obie for best play.** The mysteries of the universe, and of human and artistic creation, are explored in this award-winning play. *"Lanford Wilson's idiosyncratic SYMPATHETIC MAGIC is his BEST PLAY YET ... the rare play you WANT ... chock-full of ideas, incidents, witty or poetic lines, scientific and philosophical argument ... you'll find your intellectual faculties racing." – New York Magazine. "The script is like a fully notated score, next to which most new plays are cursory lead sheets." –The Village Voice.* [5M, 3W] ISBN: 0-8222-1630-2

**DRAMATISTS PLAY SERVICE, INC.**
440 Park Avenue South, New York, NY 10016  212-683-8960  Fax 212-213-1539
postmaster@dramatists.com  www.dramatists.com

# NEW PLAYS

- **SMASH by Jeffrey Hatcher.** Based on the novel, AN UNSOCIAL SOCIALIST by George Bernard Shaw, the story centers on a millionaire Socialist who leaves his bride on their wedding day because he fears his passion for her will get in the way of his plans to overthrow the British government. *"SMASH is witty, cunning, intelligent, and skillful."* –Seattle Weekly. *"SMASH is a wonderfully high-style British comedy of manners that evokes the world of Shaw's high-minded heroes and heroines, but shaped by a post modern sensibility."* –Seattle Herald. [5M, 5W] ISBN: 0-8222-1553-5

- **PRIVATE EYES by Steven Dietz.** A comedy of suspicion in which nothing is ever quite what it seems. *"Steven Dietz's ... Pirandellian smooch to the mercurial nature of theatrical illusion and romantic truth, Dietz's spiraling structure and breathless pacing provide enough of an oxygen rush to revive any moribund audience member ... Dietz's mastery of playmaking ... is cause for kudos."* –The Village Voice. *"The cleverest and most artful piece presented at the 21st annual [Humana] festival was PRIVATE EYES by writer-director Steven Dietz."* –The Chicago Tribune. [3M, 2W] ISBN: 0-8222-1619-1

- **DIMLY PERCEIVED THREATS TO THE SYSTEM by Jon Klein.** Reality and fantasy overlap with hilarious results as this unforgettable family attempts to survive the nineties. *"Here's a play whose point about fractured families goes to the heart, mind -- and ears."* –The Washington Post. *" ... an end-of-the millennium comedy about a family on the verge of a nervous breakdown ... Trenchant and hilarious ... "* –The Baltimore Sun. [2M, 4W] ISBN: 0-8222-1677-9

- **HONOUR by Joanna Murray-Smith.** In a series of intense confrontations, a wife, husband, lover and daughter negotiate the forces of passion, lust, history, responsibility and honour. *"Tight, crackling dialogue (usually played out in punchy verbal duels) captures characters unable to deal with emotions ... Murray-Smith effectively places her characters in situations that strip away pretense."* –Variety. *"HONOUR might just capture a few honors of its own."* –Time Out Magazine. [1M, 3W] ISBN: 0-8222-1683-3

- **NINE ARMENIANS by Leslie Ayvazian.** A revealing portrait of three generations of an Armenian-American family. *" ... Ayvazian's obvious personal exploration ... is evocative, and her picture of an American Life colored nostalgically by an increasingly alien ethnic tradition, is persuasively embedded into a script of a certain supple grace ... "* –The NY Post. *"... NINE ARMENIANS is a warm, likable work that benefits from ... Ayvazian's clear-headed insight into the dynamics of a close-knit family ... "* –Variety. [5M, 5W] ISBN: 0-8222-1602-7

- **PSYCHOPATHIA SEXUALIS by John Patrick Shanley.** Fetishes and psychiatry abound in this scathing comedy about a man and his father's argyle socks. *"John Patrick Shanley's new play, PSYCHOPATHIA SEXUALIS is ... perfectly poised between daffy comedy and believable human neurosis which Shanley combines so well ... "* –The LA Times. *"John Patrick Shanley's PSYCHOPATHIA SEXUALIS is a salty boulevard comedy with a bittersweet theme ... "* –New York Magazine. *"A tour de force of witty, barbed dialogue."* –Variety. [3M, 2W] ISBN: 0-8222-1615-9

## DRAMATISTS PLAY SERVICE, INC.
440 Park Avenue South, New York, NY 10016  212-683-8960  Fax 212-213-1539
postmaster@dramatists.com  www.dramatists.com